DEFENSE PLANNING FOR THE LATE 1990s

Studies in Defense Policy

SELECTED TITLES

DEFENSE PLANNING FOR THE LATE 1990s: BEYOND THE DESERT STORM FRAMEWORK

Michael O'Hanlon

THE BROOKINGS INSTITUTION
Washington, D.C.

Copyright © 1995
THE BROOKINGS INSTITUTION
1775 Massachusetts Avenue, N.W., Washington, D.C. 20036

All rights reserved.

Library of Congress Cataloging-in-Publication data:

O'Hanlon, Michael E.
    Defense planning for the late 1990s : beyond the Desert Storm
framework / Michael O'Hanlon.
        p.   cm.
    Includes bibliographical references.
    ISBN 0-8157-6449-9 (pbk. : alk. paper).
    1. United States—Defenses.   2. United States. Dept. of Defense—
Appropriations and expenditures.   3. United States—Politics and
government—1993–   I. Title.
    UA23.0553   1995
    355'.033'7309049—dc20   95-22189
                                                                            CIP

9 8 7 6 5 4 3 2 1

Typeset in Times Roman

Composition by Harlowe Typography Inc.,
Cottage City, Maryland

Printed by Kirby Lithographic Co.
Arlington, Virginia

*To
Cathryn*

FOREWORD

WITH a Republican Congress aiming for ways to balance the federal budget by 2002, the Pentagon has happily found itself out of range. Not only Republicans but also a large number of Democrats led by President Clinton believe that defense spending is declining enough already and it is time to look elsewhere to eliminate the deficit.

Yet the national defense budget remains at nearly 90 percent of its cold war average in real terms (roughly where the Bush administration would have kept it) at a time when the United States has the strongest military forces in history and no major adversaries. Under any of the plans now in contention on Capitol Hill—the president's, the Senate's, or the House's—defense spending will continue to decline, but will remain at 80 percent of its cold war average when the military drawdown is completed in about two years.

In this study, Michael O'Hanlon argues that the defense community should prepare for a time in the near future when pressures on the defense budget are again likely to become severe. Once cuts now proposed in medicare, medicaid, welfare, and domestic investment are translated into specific curtailments of benefits and increases in user costs, the country may resist further reductions in domestic programs, but find a balanced budget still out of reach.

The proposals set forth in this study could generate an additional $100 billion in cumulative savings beyond the president's projections over the next seven years, a significant contribution toward the roughly $1 trillion in cuts needed under most deficit elimination plans. Since the current military drawdown is slowing, policymakers could adopt these proposals without undue disruption. By the end of the decade, this alternative military posture would cost about $20 billion a year less than the administration's so-called bottom-up review force.

O'Hanlon also argues that today's defense strategy does not provide an adequate basis for U.S. security policy in the twenty-first century; at best, it is a reasonable approach to move to a new era. Its most demanding mission, engaging in two simultaneous Desert Storm–like regional conflicts against foes such as North Korea and Iraq, looks backward to the vestiges of the cold war rather than forward to the challenges of the future international order. Although residual cold war threats cannot be ignored, policymakers need to broaden the current narrow foundation for America's military role in the world. In so doing, they could produce a security doctrine and force structure better suited to the challenges of the future: in particular, the problems of civil and ethnic conflict, the need to reorient and rejuvenate the Western alliance, and the nature of relations between that alliance and other powers such as China and Russia.

Michael O'Hanlon is a research associate in the Foreign Policy Studies program at Brookings. He gratefully acknowledges the assistance of the many individuals who contributed to this effort. Special thanks go to William W. Kaufmann, Lawrence J. Korb, and John D. Steinbruner, each of whom provided unique insights and perspectives. Christina Woodward provided highly able research assistance throughout the project. Martin Binkin, Harry Dolton, Joshua M. Epstein, Lincoln Gordon, Randall Lovdahl, Michael M. Mochizuki, Janne E. Nolan, John M. Paxton, Stephen Sargeant, and Shibley Z. Telhami provided patient and thoughtful feedback and a wealth of helpful information. The author also thanks Kent Christensen, Carl Conetta, Randy DeValk, Randall Forsberg, Cathryn Garland, Tom Garwin, Charles Knight, David Mosher, William Myers, and Rachel Schmidt; he is further grateful to the members and staff of the House National Security Committee who provided reactions to an earlier form of this work when presented as congressional testimony.

The author is also indebted to Nancy D. Davidson, who edited the study, and to Lisa E. Bevell and Susan L. Woollen, who prepared it for publication. Charlotte Baldwin and Susan Blanchard provided administrative assistance.

Brookings is grateful for funding provided by the Carnegie Corporation of New York and the John D. and Catherine T. MacArthur Foundation. The views expressed in this study are those of the author and should not be ascribed to persons whose assistance is acknowledged or to the trustees, officers, or other staff members of the Brookings Institution.

BRUCE K. MAC LAURY
President

June 1995
Washington, D.C.

CONTENTS

Tables

Figures

CHAPTER ONE

THE CURRENT U.S. DEFENSE DEBATE

IS THE DEBATE about post–cold war U.S. defense policy nearly over? U.S. military strategy, forces, and budgets, although still contested within certain parameters, appear more broadly to be reaching a state of political equilibrium. The Clinton administration is only now moving below the military budgets and force levels called for by the Bush administration, and its plans ultimately would result in a military whose size and real, constant-dollar cost are only about 10 percent below those planned by the Pentagon under Secretary Dick Cheney.[1] According to current plans, the 1999 defense budget will be $239 billion (measured in 1995 dollars), in contrast to $262 billion in 1995 and $250 billion requested for 1996. By contrast, the cold war average was about $300 billion, and the 1990 level was about $350 billion (see figure 1-1). After 1999 some real increases in defense budgets are foreseen; thus annual U.S. defense spending will remain at or above 80 percent of its cold war average into the indefinite future.

If some congressional Republicans have their way, defense spending might decrease less in the next few years. The centrality of the defense issue in the Contract with America, as well as the strong criticisms of Clinton administration defense policies by Republican National Security and Armed Services Committee Chairmen Floyd Spence and Strom Thurmond, sometimes gave the impression that real increases were in the offing.[2] But fiscal pressures have now constrained both houses of Congress to suggest budgets differing by no more than a few percentage points from those now proposed by the Clinton administration.[3] By contrast, the debates of the early 1980s produced an increase of more than one-third in the cost of the U.S. military, and the debates of the early 1990s led to a cut of nearly equal proportions.

1

Figure 1-1.   Department of Defense Outlays and Budget Authority, Fiscal Years 1947–2001ª

Billions of 1995 dollars

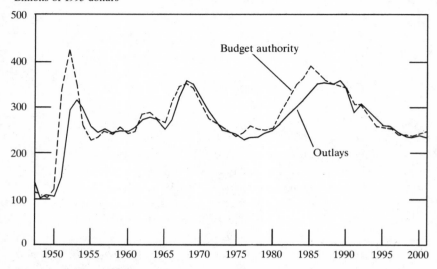

Sources: Department of Defense, *National Defense Budget Estimates for Fiscal Year 1995*; Department of Defense, "Budget Request for Fiscal Year 1966."

a. Figures do not include the costs of the Department of Energy's nuclear weapons activities, which have typically been about $10 billion a year since the mid-1980s and generally ranged from $5 billion to $10 billion a year in earlier periods dating back to 1950. For 1996–2001, figures are projected.

The Need for a Broader Debate

At first blush, defense spending within this range of new consensus does not seem unreasonable. In 1994 alone, the prospects of war in Korea and in the Persian Gulf, together with a variety of activities supporting UN resolutions and peace operations, kept the U.S. military very active and attested to the logic of planning forces for simultaneous regional engagements.[4] The sense that things are about right also seems confirmed by an examination of the military's overall immediate readiness. Readiness, defined as the ability to deploy forces quickly and then initiate combat operations promptly and effectively, can be evaluated through various quantitative measures such as operations and maintenance spending per person, the quality of recruits as indicated by test scores, the experience levels of personnel, the availability of spare parts, the state of repair of military equipment, or training time. According to most such categories, current readiness is generally good by historical standards, as confirmed not only by the overall judgments of Secretary William J. Perry and top uniformed officials of the Department of Defense but also by hard data. At the same time, there are indications that, especially in light of frequent humanitarian and peacekeeping operations, budgets for readiness have little excess capacity and are being stressed in places. This suggests that there are few dollars and forces to spare.[5]

But in another sense, the post–cold war defense budget debate is just beginning, and one should not be fooled by the temporary lull in its intensity. The coalescing of support around a specific military doctrine, force structure, and budget is remarkable for an era lacking any clear strategic rival to the United States that would provide a primary benchmark for planning. Today's military doctrine and plans focus attention on a small number of countries of moderate size and importance and treat major strategic issues as ancillary. It is proper to be concerned about U.S. interests and allies in the Korean and Southwest Asian regions. Those interests, having already been protected by the shedding of American blood, are not insignificant to the United States or its international reputation and remain at risk. By focusing so intently on those regions, however, and retaining a military posture and budget not unlike those of the cold war, the U.S. security community may fail to address potential future threats or to build constructive ties with countries like China and Russia in order to avoid drifting into adversarial relationships. It may also give insufficient weight to peace operations and related activities, as argued in the May 1995 report of the Commission on Roles and Missions of the Armed Forces.[6]

In addition, the U.S. military simply still costs more than necessary. Given strong political pressure for a balanced budget, a tax-averse public, the continually growing cost of health care, and the implications for social security of the aging of the baby boomers, further defense savings will probably be needed. Otherwise, truly serious harm to other federal priorities will be very difficult to avoid. At a time when government in general is being asked to become more efficient and streamlined, it seems reasonable—and inevitable—that the military be continually pushed to achieve those same standards as well.[7]

The Clinton administration's blueprint for U.S. defense forces through the rest of the decade, the bottom-up review (BUR) plan, will begin to require real increases in military spending at precisely the time when deficit reduction efforts will require very large cuts in overall federal

Table 1-1. The Budget Outlook, Fiscal Years 1995–2005, as of Early 1995[a]

	Deficit		Deficit without social security	
Year	Billions of dollars	Percent of GDP[b]	Billions of dollars	Percent of GDP[b]
1995	176	2.5	245	3.5
1996	207	2.8	280	3.8
1997	224	2.9	302	3.9
1998	222	2.7	306	3.7
1999	253	3.0	343	4.0
2000	284	3.1	380	4.2
2001	297	3.1	401	4.2
2002	322	3.2	433	4.3
2003	351	3.3	470	4.4
2004	383	3.5	511	4.7
2005	421	3.6	558	4.8

Source: Congressional Budget Office, *The Economic and Budget Outlook, Fiscal Years 1996-2000* (January 1995), pp. 58, 93.

a. Assumes constant real spending in discretionary accounts after 1998.

b. The average deficit in 1981-90 was 4.2 percent of GDP; not including social security, the average was 4.6 percent.

spending. The deficit would otherwise increase substantially, rising from the expected 1995 level of about $176 billion (2.5 percent of gross domestic product) to more than $320 billion (3.2 percent of GDP) by 2002 (see table 1-1).[8] This resurrection of the deficit monster would occur despite the 1990 and 1993 deficit reduction packages, which are giving inflation nearly a decade to eat away at federal discretionary spending at the same time that the economy grows by about 20 percent in real terms. Moreover, the problem is even worse if one focuses on the deficit minus the social security surplus, which currently makes the deficit appear smaller than "generational accountants" would define it.

If a balanced budget effort came fully into force around 2002 and defense took its proportionate cuts, the real defense budget would have to be cut by another $40 billion a year relative to its projected nadir in 1999. That would result in an annual budget of $200 billion in 1995 dollars. But administration and Congressional Budget Office calculations suggest that, at that point, the defense budget will instead need to be increased to at least $250 billion to sustain the BUR force.[9]

DOD officials and security policymakers should not be lulled into a sense of complacency by a political debate that seems in the short term to encourage net increases in planned defense budgets. Once the current round of defense cuts nears completion, there will be fewer economic and parochial incentives for lawmakers to oppose further budget reductions; once Bill Clinton has faced his last election in 1996, there may be fewer partisan reasons to do so as well. At that point, particularly if the Korean peninsula gradually stabilizes over the course of the 1990s, the defense budget will rise or fall much more as a function of its broad strategic underpinnings and Americans' sense of their basic place in the post–cold war world.

In this book, I outline a set of specific suggestions for U.S. military forces and budgets. Taken together, they amount to—and derive from—a significantly different strategic rationale than that espoused by the Clinton administration or its predecessor. As argued above, part of the rationale is simple frugality; I explore less expensive ways to pursue the goals of deterring regional war, conducting global military deployments, and enhancing nuclear safety.

But in a broader sense, this book seeks ways to promote a concept of cooperative security through near-term U.S. defense planning. Cooperative security, a theoretical concept developed in several previous Brookings publications, draws on ideas from international law, just war, arms control, and collective security policy. Foreign policies based on this concept would seek to expand the basic harmony of interests and security policies within the NATO alliance to a broader set of countries, would work toward a set of increasingly clear and accepted criteria for how states should go about making collective decisions on when and how to oppose threats to themselves or other countries, and would restrain the capabilities of individual states to conduct major unilateral military operations.[10]

There are problems with pushing an ambitious form of cooperative security, or certain ideas sometimes associated with it, too far or too quickly. For example, it is not clear that stable military balances can be constructed through technology and arms control, particularly in a world that is no longer bipolar. It is unlikely that all types of conflicts can be handled equally effectively by a multilateral decisionmaking process, especially in the near term, when there are often conflicts in the international community's interests in upholding human rights, national self-determination, and the territorial integrity and sovereignty of nation-states. And it is uncertain how objective rules can be constructed that allow the unambiguous assignment of blame for a given conflict in order to determine whether, and how, to become involved in trying to stop that conflict.[11]

But nevertheless there may be practical ways in which guidelines for intervention can be developed more clearly, mechanisms for conducting joint operations can be honed, and potentially threatening types of behavior can be checked. The imperative for changing the basic ways countries interact through a notion such as cooperative security seems evident at a time when growing populations, increasingly powerful weapons, and unstable politics in much of the world would seem to portend a twenty-first century that could be horribly deadly and quite dangerous. If traditional or "realist" patterns of human and national behavior go unchanged, the likely human toll—and perhaps the toll on civilization itself—could be severe. Unless there is progress in broadening the community of peaceful states, it is all too likely that traditional security institutions and ways of thinking will eventually create security dilemmas and tensions among the major powers, including emerging ones such as China.

Perhaps the greatest legacy and accomplishment of post–World War II U.S. foreign policy was the effort to help other countries rebuild economically and politically. By so doing, the United States catalyzed the creation of a community of nations, many previously adversarial, that have since become firmly convinced of each other's nonaggressive nature and produced the strongest military-political-economic bloc in world history. It is imperative that this legacy be understood and appreciated; today, there is a trend among many self-styled hawks and realists to view Western victory in the cold war primarily as a result of strong military efforts. They are right to recognize the importance of those elements, but they were only a part—and, by themselves, an insufficient part—of the successful grand strategy, which also emphasized a vision for democratic values, human rights, and economic growth.

The Clinton Administration's Strategy and Force Structure

The Clinton administration has built a military strategy and budget plan, similar to that of the Bush administration, that keeps forces and spending at somewhat more than 80 percent of average cold war levels. Its plan, again like the Bush administration's but unlike those of most cold war predecessors, focuses less on the great powers of the world than on peripheral parts of the Asian landmass where the United States has important, yet ultimately less than vital, economic and security interests.

Doctrinal Underpinnings

The Clinton administration in its bottom-up review in fact focuses even more restrictively than did the Bush administration on simultaneous wars in the Korean theater and the Persian Gulf or Mideast region. The plan holds that the United States must be capable of fighting two major wars that could break out nearly simultaneously—that is, one to three months apart, time enough for an aggressor in one theater to decide to take advantage of a U.S. military involvement somewhere else and mobilize forces for attack. Although fighting two such wars at once is considered both unlikely and undesirable, the BUR argues that to deter effectively, the United States must have the real fighting capability needed to wage that second major regional war if necessary.

These assumptions follow a straightforward logic. But the key assumption of the authors of the BUR—and the one that invites controversy—is that the military force needed to deal with a regional crisis or conflict must entail a deployment similar in size to that of Desert Storm (specifically, a force somewhat smaller than that deployed to the Persian Gulf but with roughly the same overall capabilities as a result of ongoing weapons modernization programs). Simultaneous crises or conflicts would require the capability to conduct such an operation in two theaters at once, according to the BUR. And strategic lift capabilities should be sufficiently great that they could complete the bulk of a single deployment to the first conflict before the second one developed very far.

In keeping with the limited ability and questionable willingness of major European allies to deploy substantial forces far from their own territories, the BUR assumes that not much military help would be forthcoming from the likes of Britain, France, Germany, or Japan. It assumes that any reliable allied assistance would come from only the countries directly threatened by a conflict, for example, South Korea or Saudi Arabia, Kuwait, and the other countries of the Gulf Cooperation Council (GCC). Again, in this set of assumptions, the BUR is akin to the Bush administration's plan, the so-called base force concept. But both are markedly different from cold war strategy, in which a much more serious threat to overall Western security—and directly to West European security—led to an alliance military structure in which roughly half the NATO military capability would have come from countries other than the United States.[12]

Under the Clinton administration, the pre-positioning of U.S. military equipment in the Persian Gulf and South Korean regions has been accelerated and expanded. Much of the credit for this policy must go to the Bush administration: its deft and militarily impressive handling of Saddam Hussein's threat to the region improved U.S. ties with a number of Arab states and overcame their traditional resistance to collaborating closely with a Western power. But the Clinton initiative is nevertheless a significant one. Fast sealift capability is also being expanded; taken together, the various policy initiatives will soon translate into a capability to deploy rapidly at least an additional division of ground equipment and some additional combat aircraft to the Gulf or Korea or both nearly at once. Although war could break out in other regions, it is principally in those regions of the militarized world where U.S. historical and economic interests are significant and clearly threatened.

Moreover, given the centrality of the U.S. military role in Korea and Southwest Asia, the concern about being prepared for simultaneous conflicts is principally relevant to those areas. Nowhere else in the developing world is U.S. deterrence so critical in preventing war. Thus nowhere else is it so important to avoid creating the perception of a window of vulnerability that a potential aggressor might seek to exploit because of U.S. military involvement elsewhere.

Like the base force plan, the Clinton bottom-up review posture retains traditional naval and Marine Corps missions of global forward presence. According to prevailing doctrines of forward presence, the United States should have aircraft carrier and Marine amphibious fleets sufficiently large to maintain a nearly continuous presence in three main areas: the Mediterranean Sea, the western Pacific, and the Indian Ocean or Persian Gulf area. The purposes of those forward deployments are to stake out and remind onlookers of the United States' global commitments and interests, to have forces ready for small to moderate crises in areas along the Asian littoral or contiguous to the Red and Mediterranean Seas and Persian Gulf, and to trail other countries' naval forces such as attack submarines and ballistic missile submarines for intelligence-gathering purposes. In reality, the United States has frequently let its actual overseas naval presence fall somewhat short of stated goals, and the BUR—with its active aircraft carrier fleet having one ship less than the base force—tolerates a bit more of such shortfalls than did its predecessor. But the basic pattern of forward deployment continues essentially as during the cold war, and with comparable numbers of ships, particularly in the aircraft carrier and amphibious fleets.

Table 1-2. U.S. Military Forces, Fiscal Years 1990–99

Type of force	1990	Base force plan for 1995[a]	Actual 1995	Clinton plan for late 1990s
Active Army divisions[b]	18	12	12	10
Reserve Army divisions[b]	10	6[c]	8	5
Marine expeditionary forces	3	3	3	3
Active aircraft carriers	15	12	11	11
Reserve or training aircraft carriers	1	1	1	1
Active carrier air wings	13	11	10	10
Reserve carrier air wings	2	2	1	1
Battle force ships	546	430	373	346
Active fighter wings	24	15	13	13
Reserve fighter wings	12	11	8	7
Strategic bombers (PAA)	268	176	141	154
Active-duty manpower (thousands)	2,069	1,644	1,523	1,453
Reserve manpower (thousands)	1,128	922	965	900

Source: Secretary of Defense William J. Perry, *Annual Report to the President and the Congress* (February 1995), p. 275.

a. The base force plan, the official policy of the Bush administration, would have been almost fully in place by 1995.

b. Does not include additional brigades, of which there are at present six in the active Army and twenty-two in the reserves.

c. Does not include two cadre divisions.

In terms of forces and weapons, the Clinton administration plans to prepare for regional warfighting, overseas presence, and any peace operations with a military of 10 active Army divisions, 20 tactical Air Force wings, 12 aircraft carriers, and roughly 150 long-range bombers (see table 1-2). The administration also would keep 42 additional brigades in the National Guard; a total of 110 to 116 naval surface combatants, including about 20 frigates, 25 cruisers, and some 65 to 70 destroyers; 45 to 55 attack submarines; roughly 6 imaging satellites; and some 300 P-3 maritime patrol aircraft as well as a host of other reconnaissance, electronic warfare, and command and control planes. Total forces would include roughly 1.45 million active-duty personnel, together with somewhat less than 800,000 full-time civilian staff and approximately another 900,000 reserve personnel.[13]

Major weapons acquisition programs in various stages of development or production include the C-17 transport aircraft; the F-22, F/A-18 E/F, and joint advanced strike aircraft (JAST) tactical aircraft programs; the V-22 tilt-rotor aircraft; the Arleigh Burke–class destroyer and Seawolf submarine, as well as the new attack submarine; and the advanced field artillery system. But perhaps most important of all for the era of precision-strike warfare are several classes of sensors, communications links, and advanced precision-guided munitions. These include a number of unmanned aerial vehicles (UAVs) for reconnaissance; communications systems that would allow the rapid dissemination of data acquired through UAVs, overhead satellites, and other platforms; a number of munitions for aircraft and other weapons platforms, including the sensor-fused weapon, the joint direct-attack munition, the brilliant antiarmor submunition, the sense-and-destroy-armor munition, the joint-standoff weapon, and laser-guided bombs; and all-weather day-or-night navigation and targeting capabilities for a number of tactical combat aircraft and bombers.

In the realm of nuclear weapons, the BUR and the recently released nuclear posture review (NPR) also retain a nuclear weapons targeting doctrine and force posture like that of the Bush plan. The START II agreement negotiated under President Bush is retained as a framework for planning, not only as a practical short-term posture because several years of implementation will be required to put START II fully in place, but also as a long-term guide. (Nuclear forces rendered excess by START II will be taken off alert more rapidly under the Clinton policy, however.)[14] Changes made by Bush are retained: bombers have been taken off runway alert, routine deployments of nuclear weapons on surface ships have ended, almost all tactical nuclear weapons except several hundred in Europe have been returned to the United States, and day-to-day pretargeting of ICBMs and SLBMs on Russian targets has ended.[15]

But the NPR contains no proposals for further cuts or major doctrinal changes such as a no-first-use policy, except that it does (albeit reluctantly) codify the administration's policy to pursue a multilateral ban on nuclear weapons testing. War plans, though much smaller than in recent decades, are comparable in size to the single integrated operational plans (SIOPs) of the 1960s,[16] and the overall nuclear inventory is comparable to levels of the mid-to-late 1950s.[17] The SIOP includes sites housing nuclear weapons and warheads, conventional military assets, industrial assets, and military command and control infrastructure.

U.S. nuclear weapons modernization programs, while substantially more modest than during the past fifty years, continue to emphasize improved accuracy and counterforce capability—as evidenced by continued acquisition of the Trident II D5 missile as well as the planned upgrade of Minuteman III missile guidance systems. In addition, although the United States has scaled back the Department of Energy's nuclear weapons research, development, and testing program, it continues to spend sums on these activities comparable to past levels to promote a deeper understanding of nuclear weapons physics and engineering.[18]

Under START II, the United States plans to retain the capacity to return to deployed strategic warhead levels higher than the treaty's limit of 3,000 to 3,500 as a "hedge" against undesirable political and military developments in Russia.[19] At present, START II has not been ratified by Russia or the United States, and START requires reductions only to a level of some 7,000 to 8,000 warheads by the end of the decade. With Ukraine's recent decisions to ratify START, accede to the nuclear Non-Proliferation Treaty, and return its warheads to Russia, problems among the former Soviet republics themselves may no longer put the treaty at risk. However, Russian conservatives are concerned that START II would confer too many advantages upon the United States.[20] Their concerns are amplified by U.S. strategic missile defense efforts that may still have goals inconsistent with limits in the Antiballistic Missile Treaty.[21]

The Clinton administration displays a marginally greater willingness to participate in UN peace operations than did its predecessor.[22] It broadened the Bush administration's efforts in Somalia (though the seeds for doing so were largely inherent in the original humanitarian mission), attempted a fundamental political transformation in Haiti, and tried to toughen up U.S. policy toward the Serbs in the former Yugoslavia through advocacy of the "lift and strike" strategy. However, the Clinton administration has made little sustained effort to change international policy in general and has often been reluctant to get involved in peace operations. Overall, it is probably fair to characterize the Bush and Clinton policies toward peacekeeping and peace enforcement as similar in scope and ambitiousness, if not in every specific case.

More mundanely, the Clinton administration also is devoting about $17 billion a year to "nontraditional" defense activities, principally environmental cleanup. Although the administration is often criticized for doing so, the last Bush administration budget allocated just as much for these activities, most of which are required by the legacy of the cold war (see table 1-3).

Finally, unspoken but probably present in the Clinton BUR strategy—as it was spoken yet not officially declared in Bush administration thinking—is also a desire to retain the trappings of sole superpower status,

Table 1-3. Nontraditional Defense Spending, Fiscal Years 1990–95
Billions of 1995 dollars of budget authority

Activity	Actual				Estimated	
	1990	1991	1992	1993	1994	1995
DOD environmental cleanup	1.6	2.8	4.0	5.3	5.6	5.2
Defense conversion and dual-use technology[a]	0.6	0.7	1.2	2.9	3.4	3.3
Drug interdiction and counterdrug activities	0.5	1.2	1.3	1.2	0.9	0.7
Former Soviet Union threat reduction	0	0	0.2	0.4	0.4	0.4
Humanitarian assistance	0	0	0.2	0.2	0.1	0.1
Other miscellaneous[b]	0.8	1.0	1.2	1.3	1.4	1.3
DOE environmental cleanup	2.3	3.6	4.3	5.5	5.1	5.1
DOE dual-use technology and research	0	0.1	0.1	0.2	0.2	0.2
Total	5.8	9.4	12.5	17.0	17.1	16.3

Source: Congressional Budget Office, adapted from Stephen Daggett and Keith Berner, "Items in the Department of Defense Budget That May Not Be Directly Related to Traditional Military Activities," Congressional Research Service memorandum, March 21, 1994, p. 39; *Budget of the United States Government, Fiscal Year 1996*; Congressional Budget Office, *Cleaning Up the Department of Energy's Nuclear Weapons Complex* (May 1994); and Congressional Budget Office, "The Bomb's Custodians," CBO Paper (July 1994).
a. Because of accounting changes, values for 1990–92 are not strictly comparable to those for 1993–95.
b. Includes a number of small programs that are financed primarily in the operations and maintenance title, such as funding for disaster relief.

whatever that may consist of. An international order with a sole super-power, often described as one of hegemonic stability in the international relations theory literature, is believed by many to deter other countries from perceiving and seeking to exploit power vacuums.

Budgetary Implications

The Clinton administration envisions a total defense budget for 1999 of about $266 billion, or $239 billion in 1995 dollars (see table 1-4). That annual level would be some $25 billion below the anticipated Bush administration annual level for the late 1990s, which itself represented a decline of some $85 billion from the 1990 budget (roughly $350 billion in 1995 dollars) (see table 1-5).[23]

In 1995 authorized funds for the defense functions of the Departments of Defense and Energy total $262 billion (equal to the 1994 level in nominal terms). Actual spending will be roughly $270 billion, reflecting the fact that some budget authority from previous years—when budget authority was higher than it is now—has not yet been translated into

Table 1-4. Discretionary Funding for National Defense, Fiscal Years 1994–2001
Billions of current dollars unless otherwise indicated

Budget category	Actual		Proposed					
	1994	1995[a]	1996	1997	1998	1999	2000	2001
Department of Defense (051)								
Budget authority	250.5	252.6	246.0	242.8	249.7	256.3	266.2	276.6
Outlays	269.4	260.2	250.0	246.1	244.2	249.6	257.9	261.6
Atomic energy defense activities (053) and other (054)								
Budget authority	10.9	10.9	11.8	10.6	9.9	9.9	9.9	9.9
Outlays	11.9	11.4	11.4	10.9	10.3	10.0	9.9	9.9
Total national defense (050)								
Budget authority	262.2	263.5	257.8	253.4	259.6	266.3	276.0	286.5
Percent real change from previous year	. . .	−1.9	−5.3	−4.1	−0.1	−0.2	1.1	1.2
Outlays	282.2	271.6	261.4	257.0	254.5	259.7	267.8	271.5
Percent real change from previous year	. . .	−5.4	−6.6	−4.4	−3.6	−0.6	0.6	−1.2

Sources: *Budget of the United States Government, Fiscal Year 1996,* p. 124; Perry, *Annual Report to the President and the Congress,* p. 272; and data from Congressional Budget Office.

a. Includes proposed emergency supplementals and savings proposals; congressional action has since reduced budget authority for 1995 to about $262 billion and outlays to about $270 billion.

Table 1-5. Bush and Clinton Administration Defense Budgets, Fiscal Years 1994–99
Billions of current dollars

Administration	Department of Defense budget authority[a]						
	1994	1995	1996	1997	1998	1999	Total 1994–99
Bush	262.4	263.6	262.6	266.2	274.7	283.4	1,613.0
Clinton	249.0	252.2	245.4	242.2	249.7	256.0	1,494.5
Difference	−13.4	−11.4	−17.2	−24.0	−25.0	−27.4	−118.5

Source: Stephen Daggett, "A Comparison of Clinton Administration and Bush Administration Long-Term Defense Budget Plans for FY 1994–99," Congressional Research Service, December 20, 1994. These figures were prepared before the release of the fiscal year 1996 budget request and therefore differ slightly from those in table 1-4.

a. Does not include funding for Department of Energy's national security activities.

actual outlays. The declines in defense budgets have been substantial, but to date they have occurred at a more modest pace than in past drawdowns—roughly 5 percent in dollar terms and 100,000 uniformed individuals a year, in contrast to 6 percent and nearly 200,000 individuals a year after Vietnam and even greater rates after the Korean War. The pace of the drawdown under Clinton has been comparable to what it was under Bush and is soon to slow.[24] (See table 1-6 for the pace at which the uniformed military and civilian staff are declining in size.)

Under current Clinton administration plans, defense budgets will dip

Table 1-6. Military and Civilian Personnel End Strengths, Selected Fiscal Years, 1990–99

	Thousands of personnel			Percentage change		
Organization	1990	1995	1999	1990–95	1995–99	1990–99
Active-duty military personnel[a]						
Army	751	510	495	− 32	− 3	− 34
Navy	583	442	394	− 24	− 11	− 32
Marine Corps	197	174	174	− 12	0	− 12
Air Force	539	400	390	− 26	− 2	− 28
Total[a]	2,069	1,526	1,453	− 26	− 5	− 30
Civilian personnel[b]						
Military services	930	721	665	− 22	− 8	− 28
Defense agency and other personnel	143	152	130	6	− 14	− 9
Total	1,073	873	795[c]	− 19	− 9	− 26

Source: Congressional Budget Office, "An Analysis of the Administration's Future Years Defense Program for 1995 through 1999," CBO Paper (January 1995), p. 27.

a. Excludes full-time National Guard and Reserve forces.

b. Figures for 1990 are adjusted to reflect the subsequent transfer of personnel from the military services to the Defense Exchange and Commissary Agency, the Defense Financial and Accounting Service, the Defense Information Systems Agency, the Defense Logistics Agency, and the Department of Defense Domestic and Overseas Dependents' Schools.

c. According to the administration's budget request for 1996, this number may be revised to about 750,000.

downward in 1996 and 1997. In 1998 and 1999 they will increase in nominal terms by roughly enough to keep pace with expected inflation.[25] After 1999, however, budgets would have to increase more. Just as the Bush base force plan eventually might have required annual budgets of $20 billion to $65 billion above what was forecast in that administration's fiscal plans, the Clinton administration's BUR force would be more expensive in the next decade than at the end of this one. According to the Congressional Budget Office, the added real requirements would be somewhere between $7 billion and $31 billion a year above the level projected for 1999.[26]

Some of that added spending will be needed for the simple reason that today's "procurement holiday"—the temporary respite from needing to buy many kinds of equipment, made possible by the military buildup of the 1980s—will end. Most weapons systems have lifetimes no longer than twenty to thirty years, and those purchased during the 1980s will thus begin to wear out. The lower end of the CBO range reflects an optimistic scenario in which the Department of Defense is able to buy all of its planned weapons at the prices it now expects, even though some of them are not yet sufficiently far along in development for DOD to know if this assumption will be valid. Historically, weapons have become more ex-

Figure 1-2. U.S. National Defense Spending, Fiscal Years 1947–2000ª
Percent of GDP

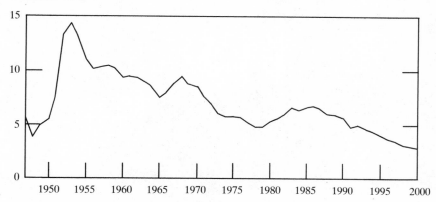

Source: DOD, *National Defense Budget Estimates for Fiscal Year 1996.*
a. Data include the DOE's nuclear activities. For 1996–2000, figures are projected.

pensive than anticipated (although to save money in that situation, policymakers would always have the recourse of curtailing or canceling a particularly expensive weapons program and buying an existing one instead). The higher estimate reflects the experience of developing past generations of new weapons, in which expected total program costs typically increased above initial estimates by one-quarter to one-half.[27]

How do these budget figures look when put into broader perspective? Unfortunately, they look different depending on the context employed; broad trends in military spending ultimately are not a particularly useful gauge of whether current and planned levels are adequate. By some measures, the extent of reductions in U.S. military spending has been great; by others, it has been modest in light of the drastically improved strategic environment. Still, even if those measures do not produce conclusive results, they are worth noting in order to provide a broad view of the defense budget debate.

At the end of the Clinton drawdown, U.S. defense spending will represent only about 3 percent of the country's GDP, in contrast to cold war levels, which ranged from roughly 5 percent to 10 percent (see figure 1-2). Already, it represents only about one-sixth of total federal spending and one-ninth of total government spending in the United States; three to four decades ago, it represented about half of federal spending and one-third of total government spending. Even at the low points of the 1970s, it represented nearly one-quarter of federal spending as well as

Figure 1-3. Global Military Expenditures, 1993
Amounts in billions of U.S. dollars

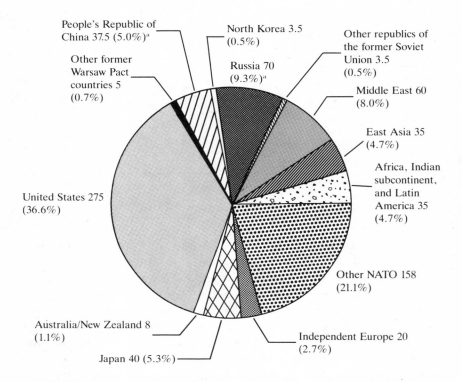

People's Republic of China 37.5 (5.0%)[a]

Other former Warsaw Pact countries 5 (0.7%)

North Korea 3.5 (0.5%)

Russia 70 (9.3%)[a]

Other republics of the former Soviet Union 3.5 (0.5%)

Middle East 60 (8.0%)

East Asia 35 (4.7%)

Africa, Indian subcontinent, and Latin America 35 (4.7%)

United States 275 (36.6%)

Other NATO 158 (21.1%)

Australia/New Zealand 8 (1.1%)

Independent Europe 20 (2.7%)

Japan 40 (5.3%)

Sources: Arms Control and Disarmament Agency, *World Military Expenditures and Arms Transfers 1991-1992* (1994); testimony of William Grundmann, Defense Intelligence Agency, before the Joint Economic Committee, June 11, 1993; and International Institute for Strategic Studies, *The Military Balance 1993-1994* (London: Brassey's, 1993).
a. Values for China and Russia are the averages of conflicting data from the above sources.

one-sixth of overall government spending.)[28] And defense procurement levels, which averaged about $100 billion a year (in 1995 dollars) during the 1980s, have dropped to about $45 billion in budget authority and $55 billion in outlays as of 1995.[29]

By other broad measures, however, U.S. defense spending remains quite substantial. Although defense spending has declined significantly in real terms, its expected level in 1999 will be roughly the same as its lower levels during the cold war era. As of 1993 the U.S. defense budget represented more than one-third of the world's total, and its GDP was one-fourth of global economic output (see figures 1-3 and 1-4). U.S. allies and close friends—principally other NATO countries and Japan, as

Figure 1-4. Distribution of Global Gross Domestic Product, 1992
Percent

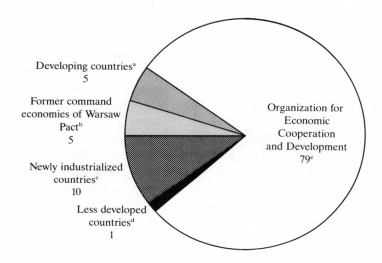

Developing countries[a]
5

Former command
economies of Warsaw
Pact[b]
5

Newly industrialized
countries[c]
10

Less developed
countries[d]
1

Organization for
Economic
Cooperation
and Development
79[e]

Sources: Congressional Budget Office, *Enhancing U.S. Security through Foreign Aid* (April 1994) p. 50; and World Bank, *World Development Report 1994* (Oxford University Press, 1994), pp. 166-67.
a. Central and South Asia, including China and India, and the Middle East.
b. Bulgaria, Czech Republic, then East Germany, Hungary, Poland, Romania, and Slovakia.
c. East Asia, South America, and Mexico.
d. Most of sub-Saharan Africa and some countries in Central America and the Caribbean.
e. Includes European Union (29 percent); United States (26 percent); Japan (16 percent); and other OECD countries (8 percent).

well as Israel, South Korea, and a handful of other smaller countries—together account for another 30 percent of global military spending and another 50 percent of world economic output. Thus all potential adversaries and neutral parties combined spend less on defense than does the United States. Indeed, most individual potential threats spend on the order of $10 billion a year, a factor of 25 less than the U.S. military. And military capabilities—as measured by a number of scoring systems that account for both quantity and quality, such as those of the Analytic Sciences Corporation—demonstrate that these raw measures of spending translate into comparable U.S. advantages in hardware.[30]

Are There Underfunding or Readiness Crises?

Late in 1994 and early in 1995, a slip in the readiness indicators of several Army divisions, together with increasing reports of strain in a

U.S. military that had been unusually busy, led to an intense debate over whether the United States was at risk of seeing its military again become "hollow." Another debate concerned the degree to which the Clinton administration's plans for defense forces and weapons exceeded the budgetary resources that same administration was planning to request over the next several years. Although the risks to the overall caliber and day-to-day preparedness of U.S. forces, and the severity of the underfunding problem, are less severe now than they were several months ago, the debates remain sufficiently recent and important to merit special consideration here.

Beginning with the issue of the funding shortfall, the Congressional Budget Office estimated in January 1995 that the Pentagon's plans could exceed likely budgetary resources by about $47 billion over the 1996–99 period. According to CBO, pay and related issues represented a total potential liability of about $25 billion over that period; net base closure costs could have been $7 billion greater than expected; unfunded peace operations might cost about $6 billion over the period; unexpected added costs in major weapons systems had the potential to add at least $8 billion; and inflation might add $20 billion more to costs. (These potential cost overruns total at least $65 billion, but the Pentagon reduced the shortfall by $18 billion in December by changing some weapons acquisition programs and receiving added funds from the president.)[31]

But roughly half of the above costs, particularly those for pay increases and growth in weapons systems costs, could be reduced by policy decisions. In addition, peacekeeping seems likely to continue being funded through supplemental appropriations, which keep Congress involved—albeit generally after the fact, but still in an important way that Congress itself seems likely to insist upon. In addition, the administration decided to make the 1995 round of base closures substantially smaller in scope than previously anticipated, reducing likely short-term costs associated with reconfiguring DOD's infrastructure. Finally, inflation estimates have been revised downward since the CBO study was released. It may thus be more appropriate to think of that shortfall as around $20 billion. Moreover, after the study was completed, the president released a budget that attempted to close that remaining gap with further cuts in procurement programs, DOE cleanup programs, and other areas.

While hardly insignificant, and unquestionably still a real concern for those involved in the annual defense budget process, any remaining shortfall thus represents 1 percent or less of the anticipated defense budget over the 1996–99 period discussed in the CBO study. Although it requires the attention of those involved in the budget process, it hardly represents a fundamental mismatch between plans and means.[32] The key matters for debate lie elsewhere: notably, in the basic premises of the BUR.

As for readiness, why did problems develop in 1994? Readiness debates are not new and are subject to a fair amount of arbitrariness. Military leaders may overreport readiness levels because doing so is consistent with their view that a defense establishment should always be prepared to do the nation's bidding, or because high levels would reflect well on them. By contrast, they may report lower than actual readiness levels if doing so seems a promising way to garner more funds for operations accounts. And in any case, readiness as defined by the Pentagon is only one component of a military force's actual capabilities at a given moment; its size, modernity, and ability to sustain prolonged operations are also critical.[33]

By overall measures, moreover, the military remains generally ready by historical standards. Relative to 1990 levels, funding for operations and maintenance will decline under the Clinton plan by almost 20 percent over the course of the decade (see table 1-7). If one subtracts the added costs of "nontraditional defense spending"—environmental cleanup, increased costs of health care, Nunn-Lugar assistance to the former Soviet republics, and defense conversion accounts that appear in the O&M category—the effective cuts would be another $4 billion. Thus scheduled reductions in O&M funding amount to about 25 percent of the 1990 base. But, by comparison personnel reductions are slated to be roughly one-third, and most cuts in force structure as much or more.

Thus, by broad measures, it is not immediately apparent why a readiness problem should have developed during this drawdown. Real spending was $48,000 per active-duty member, higher than during any year of the 1980s. Even when the above-mentioned growth in costs of health care, environmental cleanup, and certain other activities is subtracted, per-member spending was comparable to the highest levels of the 1980s, roughly $45,000 per person (see figure 1-5).[34] The uncompleted process of closing bases and reconfiguring infrastructure may make the military less efficient than during its days of a more constant size, requiring higher per capita O&M funding levels, as discussed in further detail below. But overall spending indicators are favorable.

Many key indicators of military capability and readiness are comparable to or better than levels of the late 1980s or early 1990s (see figure

Table 1-7. The Clinton Administration's Plan for Defense Department Budgets, by Title, Fiscal Years 1995–99

Billions of 1995 dollars of budget authority

Title	1990[a]	1995	1996	1997	1998	1999	Real percentage change 1990–95	Real percentage change 1995–99
Operations and support								
Military personnel	91	70	67	64	63	62	− 22	− 11
Operations and maintenance	101	93	89	86	83	83	− 8	− 11
Subtotal	192	163	156	150	146	145	− 15	− 11
Investment								
Procurement[b]	94	44	38	41	47	48	− 53	9
Research, development, test, and evaluation	42	36	33	31	29	28	− 14	− 22
Military construction	6	5	6	4	4	4	− 15	− 20
Subtotal	142	85	77	76	80	80	− 40	− 6
Family housing	4	3	4	4	4	4	− 9	10
Other adjustments	− 1	*	1	*	*	*	. . .	. . .
Total	337	252	239	229	230	230	− 25	− 9

Sources: Department of Defense, "Budget Request for Fiscal Year 1996"; and CBO, "An Analysis of the Administration's Future Years Defense Program for 1995 through 1999," p. 19.

*Less than $500 million.

a. The values for 1990 do not include costs of Operation Desert Shield.

b. Includes National Defense Sealift Fund over the 1995–99 period.

1-6 and table 1-8). Accident levels are down, even after taking into account tragedies in 1994 involving a transport aircraft at Pope Air Force Base and transport helicopters over Iraq.[35] Problems have developed in some areas; for example, in late fiscal year 1994, three Army divisions in the United States fell to so-called C-3 levels (on a scale of 1 to 4, where 1 is best), implying a capability for many but not most missions, and two divisions in Europe fell to C-2 from C-1.[36] But most such problems, not without recent precedent, are being corrected with the infusion of 1995 funds.[37]

Not all strains and shortages in the military are easily addressed by funding. The high pace of nontraditional military operations has required flexibility and stamina on the part of personnel. The men and women of the U.S. armed forces have in recent years generally proved willing, able, and proud to perform at high levels of competence across a very wide range of activities: high-intensity combat operations in Desert Storm, moderate-intensity military operations, protection of civilians against armed attack in Bosnia and Iraq, and nation building in Haiti.[38] But

Figure 1-5. Spending on Operations and Maintenance, 1979–94

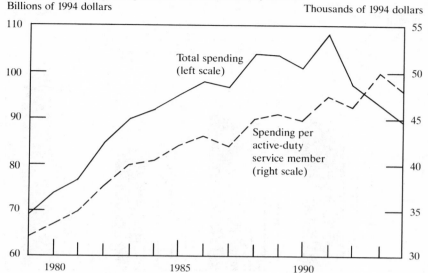

Source: Congressional Budget Office, *Trends in Selected Indicators of Military Readiness, 1980–1993*, (March 1994), pp. 37, 39.

demands on certain units have sometimes been a bit excessive, causing strains in family life, lessened readiness for traditional military missions, and a general fatigue that seems unlikely to be sustainable indefinitely.[39] Some of them will diminish naturally as the process of reconfiguring the military for the post–cold war world nears completion; others may not. Much of the alternative defense approach discussed in subsequent chapters is intended to ease remaining hardships in light of the fact that many of the nontraditional missions now being performed probably will, and should, be carried out with some frequency in the future.

Having commented favorably on the overall state of military readiness, I should note that in 1994 the Pentagon and its civilian leadership were in accord with critics that readiness problems had developed. The official Pentagon position was that the problems occurred because of unexpected expenditures, ultimately funded in two supplemental appropriations for the added marginal costs of unexpected contingency operations in the Caribbean, near and over Bosnia, over Iraq, in Kuwait, and near Somalia (see table 1-9). Because those supplementals were not submitted by the administration or approved by Congress immediately, these costs needed

Figure 1-6. Active-Duty Enlisted Personnel with More Than Four Years of Service, Selected Years, 1982–93

Percent

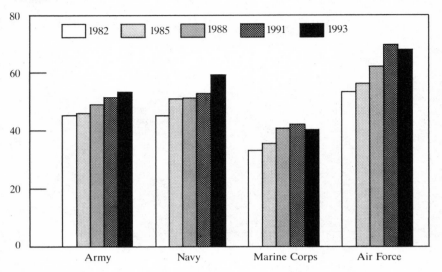

Source: CBO, *Trends in Selected Indicators of Military Readiness, 1980–1993*, p. 29.

to be paid temporarily out of flexible and partially flexible operations and maintenance accounts that totaled $47 billion for the year—largely funds used for training and related activities. By the last quarter of that fiscal year, only about $10 billion was available in such accounts; taking on the order of $1 billion or more from them thus had an obvious effect on the activities they were intended to fund (see table 1-10).

As noted earlier, the fact that DOD is reducing its force more quickly than its infrastructure raises concerns that much O&M money is being used inefficiently. It has historically been true that about half of DOD's operating costs have varied directly with force structure and half have been more or less fixed, at least in the near term and for small changes in the size of the military.[40] That is, for the sake of illustration, if the Air Force had an operations and maintenance budget of roughly $20 billion for its conventional fighter forces, and those forces were reduced by 10 percent, O&M costs might be expected to decline by only 5 percent, or roughly $1 billion, in the first year or two until infrastructure was streamlined. By that logic, an overall reduction in DOD forces of roughly 35 percent might be expected, at least in the near term, to yield O&M savings of some 15 to 20 percent.

Table 1-8. Readiness Indicators, Selected Years, 1980–93

Indicator	1980	1985	1990	1993
Aircraft "cannibalization" actions (rate per flying hours)				
Air Force	2.8	2.6	2.4	1.0
Navy	12	9	11	10.8
Quality of enlisted recruits to the active-duty military[a]	30	52	62	63
Percentage of units reporting C-1 or C-2 ratings overall[b]				
Air Force	63	81	90	92
Navy aviation index	34	90	100	81
Navy surface ships index	55	86	78	79
Marine Corps	70	75	72	67
Air Force Reserve	n.a.	48	95	92
Air Force Guard	n.a.	58	94	95
Marine Corps Reserve	n.a.	25	51	37

Source: Congressional Budget Office, "Trends in Selected Indicators of Military Readiness, 1980–1993," CBO Paper (March 1994), pp. 24, 51, 68.

n.a. Not available.

a. The services define quality of new enlistees in terms of their level of education and how well they score on the Armed Forces Qualification Test (AFQT).

b. C-ratings are readiness indicators based on a comparison of the resources units have with the levels prescribed for wartime. Army figures are classified.

Table 1-9. Costs of Unexpected U.S. Military Operations, Fiscal Years 1994 and 1995

Millions of U.S. dollars

Country	1994	1995
Bosnia	279	311.9
Cuba	107	370.1
Haiti	396	591.6
Korea	70	59.0
Rwanda	127	17.2
Somalia	520	17.3
Southwest Asia		
Provide Comfort	92	122.5
Southern Watch	332	456.4
Vigilant Warror	. . .	461.6
Equipment replenishment and related	. . .	148.1
Total	1,923	2,556

Source: Perry, *Annual Report to the President and the Congress*, pp. 39, 40.

Table 1-10. Defense Department Operations and Maintenance Budget, Fiscal Year 1995

Billions of current dollars

Purpose of funds	
Limited spending flexibility[a]	20
Guard/reserves	6
Contract services/other	5
Drug interdiction	1
Recruiting/training	3
Support activities	5
Flexibility[a]	27
Operations and deployments	22
Depot maintenance	5
No flexibility	45
Civilian pay and benefits	23
Health program	10
Environmental cleanup	4
Utilities/rents	3
Mobilization/other	5

Source: Perry. *Annual Report to the President and the Congress*. p. 42.

a. Can be shifted to a purpose other than that for which they were appropriated. though not necesarily without military consequences.

Because some economies are already being realized as bases are closed, however, the problem is probably not so severe. About 10 percent of the base structure existing at the end of the cold war has now been closed down or realigned substantially (and another 10 percent has been designated for elimination over the next few years).[41] Thus readiness per capita spending might need to be 5 percent to 10 percent higher than before to achieve the same results: about $2,000 to $4,000 a year per active-duty service member. A smaller increase would leave effective readiness funding quite good, even if not at an outright historic high.[42]

In its December defense funding decision and 1996 budget request, the administration decided to increase readiness funding levels by about $4,000 per active-duty member in comparison with 1994 levels. Such an increase should be sufficient and may explain why the individual service chiefs reportedly consider the 1996 budget proposal adequate.[43]

The Clinton administration and its predecessor deserve credit: they have effected a major military drawdown without doing damage to the remaining force or traditional U.S. security commitments. And they have begun to wrestle with the new challenges of peace operations, complex humanitarian interventions, and military-to-military relations and joint activities with countries that previously were potential adversaries. But it is time to establish firmer underpinnings needed to address the likely security challenges of the next century.

Notes

1. Congressional Budget Office, "An Analysis of the President's February Budgetary Proposals," CBO Paper (March 1993), p. IV-3; and Congressional Budget Office, *Enhancing U.S. Security through Foreign Aid* (April 1994), p. 70.

2. See, for example, Bill Gertz, "Incoming Chairmen Pledge to Beef Up Defense Budgets," *Washington Times*, November 11, 1994, p. 12.

3. See, for example, "Comparison of the Clinton, Domenici, and Kasich Defense Spending Plans," Defense Budget Project, Washington, May 12, 1995; Philip Finnegan, "Republicans Eye Conversion, Peacekeeping Cuts," *Defense News*, November 14–20, 1994, p. 1; Keith Berner and Stephen Daggett, "Items in FY 1995 Defense Legislation That May Not Be Directly Related to Traditional Military Capabilities," Congressional Research Service memorandum, October 31, 1994; and Office of Senator John McCain, "Restoring an Effective Defense: Key Areas for Action," December 1994.

4. For an official statement of this view, see Secretary of Defense William J. Perry, "What Readiness to Fight Two Wars Means," letter to the editor, *New York Times*, February 16, 1995, p. A26.

5. Congressional Budget Office, "Trends in Selected Indicators of Military Readiness, 1980–1993," CBO Paper (March 1994); letter from Secretary of Defense William J. Perry to Honorable John Murtha, Chairman, Subcommittee on Defense, House Committee on Appropriations, November 15, 1994; and Michael A. Dornheim, "Fogleman to Stress 'Stability' after Deep Cuts," *Aviation Week and Space Technology*, November 7, 1994, p. 28.

6. For another perspective on the potential pitfalls of focusing exclusively on current military demands, see Richard K. Betts, *Military Readiness: Concepts, Choices, Consequences* (Brookings, 1995). The Roles and Missions report is described in Eric Schmitt, "New Report on Long-Sought Goal: Efficiency in Military," *New York Times*, May 25, 1995, p. B13; and Bradley Graham, "Study Panel Outlines a Streamlined Military," *Washington Post*, May 25, 1995, p. A23.

7. Before the 1994 congressional elections, well-known forecasters were predicting defense budgets in the range of $205 billion early in the next century, measured in constant 1995 dollars. Clearly, the elections have changed the defense budget environment somewhat, at least temporarily. But broad structural issues—a tight budget, a lack of major strategic foe, and a public that is unwilling to tolerate American casualties in many types of overseas conflicts—are likely to outlast the current situation, in which a president seen as vulnerable on defense issues is pressured by his political opponents to spend more on the military. See, for example, "EIA Charts Show Gradual Decline in DOD Budget," *Aerospace Daily*, October 13, 1994, p. 61.

8. The president's 1996 budget effectively calls for a nominal freeze in discretionary spending, for 1999 and 2000, which if continued through 2005 could reduce that year's deficit by $145 billion. However, it does not seem judicious to assume such real savings without a detailed and widely accepted plan for how they would be made.

9. Congressional Budget Office, "An Analysis of the Administration's Future Years Defense Program for 1995 through 1999," CBO Paper (January 1995), p. 50; and presentation by William Lynn, director, Program Analysis and Evaluation, Department of Defense, at the Brookings Institution, April 4, 1995.

10. See, for example, Janne E. Nolan, "The Concept of Cooperative Security," in Janne E. Nolan, ed., *Global Engagement: Cooperation and Security in the 21st Century* (Brookings, 1994), p. 5.

11. See Richard K. Betts, "Systems for Peace or Causes of War? Collective Security, Arms Control, and the New Europe," *International Security*, vol. 17 (Summer 1992), pp. 5–43; and statement of Barry R. Posen, in *The Use of Force in the Post-Cold War Era*, Hearings before the House Committee on Armed Services, 103 Cong. 1 sess. (Government Printing Office, 1993).

12. Congressional Budget Office, *U.S. Ground Forces and the Conventional Balance in Europe* (June 1988), pp. 93–97.

13. Secretary of Defense William J. Perry, *Annual Report to the President and the Congress* (February 1995), p. 275.

14. See Thomas W. Lippman, "Nations Agree to Accelerate Arsenal Cuts," *Washington Post*, September 29, 1994, p. A26.

15. Department of Defense, "Nuclear Posture Review," 1994.

16. Desmond Ball, "The Development of the SIOP, 1960–1983," in Desmond Ball and Jeffrey Richelson, eds., *Strategic Nuclear Targeting* (Cornell University Press, 1986), pp. 66–70; and David Alan Rosenberg, "The Origins of Overkill: Nuclear Weapons and American Strategy, 1945–1960," in Steven E. Miller, ed., *Strategy and Nuclear Deterrence* (Princeton University Press, 1984), pp. 116–17.

17. See Thomas B. Cochran, William M. Arkin, and Milton M. Hoenig, *Nuclear Weapons Databook*, vol. 1: *U.S. Nuclear Forces and Capabilities* (Cambridge, Mass.: Ballinger, 1984), p. 14; Congressional Budget Office, *Implementing START II* (March 1993), p. 13; and Congressional Budget Office, *The START Treaty and Beyond* (October 1991), p. 36.

18. Congressional Budget Office, "The Bomb's Custodians," CBO Paper (July 1994), pp. 2, 4–5.

19. DOD, "Nuclear Posture Review," 1994.

20. See, for example, "Officials Predict START II Will Be Shot Down in Russian Parliament," *Inside the Pentagon*, December 22, 1994, p. 2.

21. Congressional Budget Office, "The Future of Theater Missile Defense," CBO Paper (June 1994), pp. 47–62.

22. For a balanced and up-to-date expression of Clinton administration thinking on peace operations, see President William J. Clinton, *A National Security Strategy of Engagement and Enlargement* (Executive Office of the President, February 1995), pp. 16–17.

23. CBO, "An Analysis of the President's February Budgetary Proposal," p. IV-4; Congressional Budget Office, *An Analysis of the President's Budgetary Proposals for Fiscal Year 1995* (April 1994), p. 32; and Congressional Budget Office, "Planning for Defense: Affordability and Capability of the Administration's Program," CBO Memorandum (March 1994), p. 1.

24. For a good overview of these trends, see Rachel Schmidt, "Economic Adjustment to Disarmament: Recent U.S. Experiences," in James Brown, ed., *New Horizons and Challenges in Arms Control and Verification* (Amsterdam: VU University Press, 1994), p. 250.

25. *Budget of the United States Government, Fiscal Year 1995*, p. 225; and CBO, *Enhancing U.S. Security through Foreign Aid*, p. 70.

26. See Congressional Budget Office, "Fiscal Implications of the Administration's Proposed Base Force," CBO Staff Memorandum (December 1991), pp. 1–5; and CBO, "An Analysis of the Administration's Future Years Defense Program for 1995 though 1999," p. 50.

27. The increases in costs would be up to $10 billion in the Army, $13 billion in the Navy, and $4 billion a year in the Air Force, according to earlier and more detailed Congressional Budget Office reports. See "The Costs of the Administration's Plan for the Navy through the Year 2010," "The Costs of the Administration's Plan for the Army through the Year 2010," and "The Costs of the Administration's Plan for the Air Force through the Year 2010," CBO Memorandums (November 1994).

28. Office of the Comptroller of the Department of Defense, *National Defense Budget Estimates for FY 1995* (March 1994), pp. 154–55, 160–61.

29. Ibid., pp. 85–97.

30. See Congressional Budget Office, "Assessing Future Trends in the Defense Burdens of Western Nations," CBO Paper (April 1993), p. viii. The U.S. military personnel level of roughly 1.45 million will be comparable in size to Russia's, slightly greater than India's, North Korea's, or Vietnam's, and half that of China.

31. CBO, *An Analysis of the President's Budgetary Proposals for Fiscal Year 1995*, pp. 32–34; letter from Senators John McCain and John Warner to colleagues, December 5, 1994; statement of Robert F. Hale, assistant director, National Security Division, Congressional Budget Office, before the House Committee on Armed Services, March 19, 1991, pp. 15–18; CBO, "Planning for Defense," p. 14; and General Accounting Office, *Future Years Defense Program: Optimistic Estimates Lead to Billions in Overprogramming*, NSIAD-94-210 (July 1994), pp. 5–8.

32. Spending for activities such as environmental cleanup, aid to the former Soviet republics, and the drug war, while also driving up needed levels of funding for operations and maintenance, is relatively easy to identify in the budget and thus—unless knowingly underfunded—less likely to be the cause of unanticipated funding shortfalls. Indeed, it is the very presence of these activities in the budget that has heightened their visibility and contentiousness. See Berner and Daggett, "Items in FY 1995 Defense Legislation."

33. Lawrence J. Korb, "The Readiness Gap: What Gap?" *New York Times Magazine*, February 26, 1995, pp. 40–41; and Bradley Graham, "Army Clarifies Historical Context of Readiness Alarm," *Washington Post*, January 13, 1995, p. A15.

34. CBO, "Planning for Defense," pp. 1, 7, 8; Michael O'Hanlon, *The Art of War in the Age of Peace* (Westport, Conn.: Praeger, 1992), pp. 34–35; and CBO, "Trends in Selected Indicators of Military Readiness, 1980–1993," pp. 38–40.

35. CBO, "Trends in Selected Indicators of Military Readiness, 1980–1993"; *Department of the Navy 1994 Posture Statement* (1994); and data supplied by military services. There were roughly 175 on-duty operational fatalities in 1994.

36. Rick Atkinson, "U.S. Troops in Europe Slip in Readiness," *Washington Post*, December 8, 1994, p. A40.

37. See Eric Schmitt, "Ready for Combat? The Assessment Isn't Simple," *New York Times*, December 20, 1994, p. B7.

38. See, for example, Merrie Schilter Lowe, "Troops Not Complaining, Campanale Says," *Air Force News Service*, November 29, 1994.

39. Letter of Senators McCain and Warner; and Capt. Mike Pierson, "Stress Affects Flying and Families," ACC News, November 30, 1994.

40. CBO, "Planning for Defense," p. 15.

41. Office of the Secretary of Defense, Base Closure and Utilization Desk, "Major Base Closure Summary," October 26, 1994.

42. Over time, O&M spending tends to increase due to the increasing technological sophistication of weaponry, but such concerns do not matter greatly over a short period—especially if, as today, procurement of new weapons is occurring at only a modest pace. See Steven M. Kosiak, "Analysis of the Fiscal Year 1996 Defense Budget Request," Defense Budget Project, Washington, March 1995.

43. See interview with Secretary of Defense William J. Perry, *Air Force Times*, January 2, 1995, p. 40.

CHAPTER TWO

AN ALTERNATIVE DEFENSE
POSTURE AND BUDGET

COLD WAR grand strategy led to the creation of German and Japanese self-defense forces and the NATO alliance. But the Clinton administration's military strategy does little to strengthen, ally with, defend, or counter any of the famous "five centers" of global industrial activity that George Kennan identified in 1948.[1] Nor does it reflect any logical successor to that geopolitical framework. For example, it might have added China to the list of major centers or viewed the insidious dangers of civil and ethnic conflict and rapid population growth around the world as a major security issue for the United States. Rather, the bottom-up review—like the base force and associated national security strategy before it—centers most of its attention on a small number of countries that are generally of modest economic and geopolitical importance to the United States, representing less than 5 percent of the world's population and aggregate GDP.

The historical and humanitarian ties that bind the United States to South Korea and Israel have important and unique features, to be sure, and the Western world's dependence on Persian Gulf oil exceeds its economic reliance on any other major resource found in developing countries. But it hardly follows that other countries and interests should be treated as relatively unimportant or that U.S. interests in Korea and Southwest Asia are strategically vital in the proper sense of the word.

To be sure, the United States and its close allies must remain vigilant in those theaters where long-standing interests and allies still face fairly acute—though only modestly capable—threatening forces. But they must also continue to find ways to address insidious threats exacerbated by political instability, economic stagnation, overpopulation, and weapons proliferation in some of the poorer developing countries. In addition, they must attempt to build constructive security relationships with great powers that are not yet allies but also are not adversaries, most notably China and Russia. It is also imperative to develop, through multilateral discussion as well as real-world practical experience, guidelines about when force can and cannot be used, what level of force should be employed, and what mechanisms can allow collaboration among the major powers in substantial military actions.

A Strategy for Transition

Some parts of the above agenda will require more time than others. But certain steps could be taken promptly. First, U.S. citizens and policymakers could recognize that, just as the secretary of defense has himself said on occasion, actually waging two large-scale tactically offensive regional wars at once, and without any substantial help from the major allies, is implausible.[2] But it is not the right mission anyway. In the two theaters where a large-scale U.S. military engagement in a regional conflict is plausible, deterrence theory would suggest that the enduring character of U.S. military and political involvement make a major conflict quite unlikely. Military planning should focus on reinforcing this desirable state of deterrence and, if necessary, waging combat operations early in the course of a conflict, rather than planning to retake lost territory with large forces later on.

An improved ability to deploy to those theaters rapidly with some ground units and a sizable air capability should, when coupled with the forces of regional allies, provide ample deterrence. Crudely put, U.S. military strategy for regional warfare could shift from the Desert Storm model to the Desert Shield model, building on the experience of the 200,000 U.S. troops deployed in 1990 to defend Saudi Arabia from any possible Iraqi attack rather than the 500,000 later deployed to liberate Kuwait. The goal would be, through rapid deployment, to deter regional conflicts and, if necessary, to prosecute one or two of them—primarily from the air and largely if not exclusively over the territory of the adversary. U.S. military capabilities in transport, rapid deployability, and prepositioning would be expanded further under this policy. But active ground forces could be cut back by roughly two divisions, reserve ground forces by roughly six division-equivalents, and tactical combat aircraft by nine wings (counting Navy, Marine, and Air Force elements) from the proposed BUR force.

Such a force structure would retain the ability to expand one of the Desert Shield–like operations into a Desert Storm. Doing so could be necessary for a regional war in Korea or Southwest Asia that unfolded disastrously for the United States or for a conflict somewhere else where rapid responsiveness was implausible and the United States would not necessarily have a Desert Shield option. The BUR suggests that such a war could require four to five Army divisions, four to five Marine expeditionary brigades, four to five aircraft carriers, ten wings of tactical combat aircraft, one hundred heavy bombers, and some reserve military elements. Under my proposed alternative, all of those forces could be provided at the same time that a second operation, akin to Desert Shield, was conducted elsewhere.

Second, the United States could also conclude that fighting regional wars does not require major weapons modernization programs, particularly for advanced air-to-air fighters, stealth bombers, quiet attack submarines, or tilt-rotor aircraft. As argued by Admiral William Owens, vice chairman of the Joint Chiefs of Staff, the emphasis in modernization for an age of precision-strike warfare should be on sensors and munitions.[3]

Third, U.S. policymakers could decide that in an era that lacks any major strategic threat to the United States—but nevertheless is dangerous by virtue of the spread of weapons of mass destruction, precision-guided delivery vehicles, and international political movements that resort to terrorism—nuclear weapons endanger U.S. security more than they contribute to it. By that line of reasoning, nuclear weapons have no role in U.S. security policy except to deter the use of weapons of mass destruction by some other country. Consistent with this view are further cuts in offensive forces, a permanent end to nuclear testing, enhanced controls over fissile materials and warheads in countries that possess them, and no large deployment of strategic defenses unless they are, through negotiation, made consistent with efforts to reduce nuclear offensive weaponry.

Fourth, the country could also recognize that its military role in multilateral peace operations—be it as a direct participant or as guarantor, backup, or extractor of other countries' troops—has taken on the purpose traditionally associated with naval and Marine forward-presence operations: showing the U.S. flag and proving U.S. commitment to the security of various regions and countries. Thus routine forward presence can be scaled back sharply. Occasional naval exercises and ship deployments, as well as crisis response when necessary, could make possible a cut of roughly one-third in the Navy carrier fleet and a more tolerable pace of activity for the Marines.

Finally, U.S. citizens and policymakers could determine that many peace operations have some potential relevance to long-term U.S. security, albeit not enough direct linkage to justify frequent direct American involvement. For situations such as the 1994 genocide in Rwanda, the United States and other Western militaries, as well as those of Russia, China, and other powers, need to work under UN auspices to help prepare other countries' forces to share future responsibilities for such missions. The United Nations and its member states should also improve the financial mechanisms available to help countries hurt by sanctions against neighbors or attempting to rebuild physically and politically after years of warfare. Giving greater priority to peace operations and conflict resolution in official security policy would also provide a concrete mechanism to engage China and Russia more actively in future international security relationships so that they will not be so likely to perceive NATO and other associations as directed against them.[4]

At the same time, peace operations are important enough to U.S. interests that they should not necessarily have to be ended during simultaneous regional crises. Roughly two light division-equivalents should therefore remain in the active U.S. force structure above and beyond what a "Desert Shield plus Desert Storm" requirement would dictate. Those forces would only be called upon for regional warfighting if a conflict went badly at first and a response even greater than the BUR anticipates for a full-fledged major regional conflict was required in one of the theaters.

I explore and specify the consequences of such a change in strategy for force structure, operations, and weapons acquisition policy, as well as UN peace operations, in the rest of this book.

Costs and Savings of the Alternative Defense Posture

The suggested alternative, once phased in by 1999, would make cuts of about $27 billion a year relative to the plans of the Clinton administration. But it would also add several billion dollars a year in funding, yielding a net annual savings of nearly $20 billion, or roughly 8 percent. In contrast to the administration's plan to provide $239 billion in budget authority for 1999, the alternative would cost about $220 billion in 1999, measured in constant 1995 dollars, or $266 billion versus $245 billion in nominal terms.

It is useful to place these broad numbers in context. A number of alternative defense strategies and budgets were proposed in the early 1990s. In 1993 the Henry Stimson Center released a major report suggesting annual defense budgets of around $210 billion in 1995 dollars. A year earlier, House Armed Services Committee Chairman Les Aspin laid out four alternatives for defense ranging from $210 billion a year to about $268 billion in 1995 dollars (with intermediate options at $225 billion and $245 billion). Finally, in a previous Brookings defense volume, William Kaufmann and John Steinbruner laid out three defense options estimated to cost roughly $170 billion, $195 billion, and $230 billion over the long term.[5] Thus the alternative I lay out here would fall in the middle of a range of budgets suggested by a number of thoughtful analysts over the last few years, which is of course neither a qualifying nor disqualifying characteristic.

Nearly 45 percent of the alternative's gross savings in the year 1999 would be in the Department of the Navy (though about $2 billion of that money, or 7 percent of the DOD total, is attributable to the Marine Corps). Slightly more than 20 percent of the gross savings are in the Army and slightly less than 20 percent in the Air Force, about 3 percent are in the Department of Energy, and about 15 percent are found in defensewide programs.

Specifically, the largest savings in the Navy would come from cuts in the aircraft carrier force and associated escort vessels and air wings, procurement of DDG-51 destroyers, the size of the ballistic missile and attack submarine fleets, and the Trident missile program. Marine Corps reductions would result from cancellation of the V-22 aircraft and elimination of longer-range tactical aircraft from the force structure. Air Force cuts would center on cancellation of the F-22 fighter program but also include a reduction in tactical combat wings by two and a scaling back of the Minuteman III missile fleet to one hundred missiles, as well as cancellation of the missile guidance upgrade program. Army retrenchments would focus, by contrast, on force structure. Specifically, the active Army would lose one active heavy combat division and one active light division-equivalent. The Army National Guard would retain the fifteen brigades designated for enhanced readiness status, but scale back the size of all other brigades to battalion size, which translates into a two-thirds

Table 2-1. Major Differences between the Clinton Administration's Plan and an Alternative Defense Posture, Fiscal Year 1999

Category	Administration's BUR plan	Suggested alternative	Approximate annual savings (billions of 1995 dollars)
	Suggested cuts		
Operating and support costs			
Active Army divisions	10	8	4
Army National Guard division-equivalents	14	8	2
Air Force tactical combat wings	20	18	0.7
Marine Corps fighter wing-equivalents	5	2	1
Navy aircraft carrier battle groups and air wings[a]	12/11	8/7	4
Air Force Minuteman missiles	450–500	100	1.25
Navy attack submarines	45–55	35	1
Trident Missiles submarines	14	9	0.5
Weapons acquisition			
Air Force F-22 fighter	440	0	3
Marine Corps V-22 aircraft	425	0	1
Navy DDG-51 destroyer	Buy 16 more	Buy 8 more	3
Navy D5 Trident II missile	432	337	1
Other activities			
Department of Energy nuclear weapons labs and other facilities	3 labs, 5,000 or more warheads	2.5 labs, 3,500 or fewer warheads	0.5
Communications and intelligence	Sustain average level of 1980s	Make modest further cuts	3
DOD medicine	Retain service-based system	Rely more on HMO usage and copay-ments; close USUHS	0.4
Subtotal	. . .	. . .	27

cut in the personnel, cost, and capabilities of the remaining twenty-seven combat brigades. Thus the Guard would be reduced from roughly fourteen division-equivalents to eight, cuts comparable to those recently recommended by the congressionally mandated Commission on Roles and Missions of the Armed Forces (see table 2-1 for details of the specific cuts).

Partly balancing the above savings would be increases within each department. They would be concentrated in the Air Force, notably in its

Table 2-1 (continued)

Category	Administration's BUR plan	Suggested alternative	Approximate annual savings (billions of 1995 dollars)
Suggested increases			
Marine Corps pre-positioned brigade sets[b]	3	4	−0.5
Army pre-positioned brigade sets[b]	4	6	−1
Air Force pre-positioned munitions, support equipment, fuel[b]	Modest	Enough for 2-week war	−1
Navy fast sealift capacity	2 divisions	3 divisions	−0.3
Air Force 747-Class airlift	0	100	−2.25
Air Force KC-10 tankers or equivalent	60	120	−1
Air Force F-15 aircraft	200	400	−1
Marine CH-46/CH-53 helicopter or equivalent	0	375	−0.5
UN training and equipment programs	0	2 centers; 15 brigades	−0.3
Subtotal	...	...	−8
Overall defense budget			
Total national defense (050)	...	...	19[c]

Sources: Congressional Budget Office, "Options for Reconfiguring Service Roles and Missions," CBO Paper (March 1994); Congressional Budget Office, "Implications of Additional Reductions in Defense Spending" (October 1991), p. 16; Congressional Budget Office, *Structuring U.S. Forces after the Cold War: Costs and Effects of Increased Reliance on the Reserves* (September 1992), p. 8; Congressional Budget Office, *Enhancing U.S. Security through Foreign Aid* (April 1994), pp. 65–76; Congressional Budget Office, *Reducing the Deficit: Spending and Revenue Options* (February 1995), pp. 11–98; Congressional Budget Office, *The START Treaty and Beyond* (October 1991), p. 140; *Budget of the United States Government, Fiscal Year 1996*, pp. 121–28; Steven M. Kosiak, "Analysis of the Fiscal Year 1996 Defense Budget Request," Defense Budget Project, Washington, March 1995, p. 17 and table 10; and General Accounting Office, *Military Afloat Prepositioning: Wartime Use and Issues for the Future*, NSIAD 93-39 (November 1992), p. 8.

a. Associated with the reduction in carrier battle groups would be a reduction in the fleet of major surface combatants—cruisers, destroyers, and frigates—to 100 ships rather than the BUR's planned level of 110 to 116.

b. In or near Korea and Southwest Asia.

c. The BUR would require $239 billion in budget authority for the 050 account in 1999; the alternative, $220 billion (in 1995 dollars).

procurement budgets for airlift and tanker aircraft, F-15E ground-attack aircraft, and pre-positioned munitions, fuel, and equipment. Overall, Air Force spending would increase by more than $5 billion a year over the next ten years in these areas, completely offsetting the cuts in its budget specified above. Modest Navy spending increases would fund ships for pre-positioning and fast sealift; the Marine Corps would procure substitute helicopters for the CH-46 and CH-53 fleets in lieu of acquiring the V-22; and the Army would maintain two additional brigade sets of pre-positioned equipment.

The $19 billion in net savings in budget authority, with more than $15 billion in personnel and operations and maintenance categories, would translate into about $17 billion in outlay savings by 1999.[6] The Clinton plan envisions outlays of about $233 billion in 1999, measured in 1995 dollars ($260 billion in nominal terms); the alternative would entail outlays of about $216 billion (about $241 billion nominally).

The first year when the alternative posture's cuts would be fully phased in is 1999. They would be made gradually enough (about 50,000 uniformed personnel a year, in contrast to an average of 100,000 a year earlier in the decade) to avoid undue disruption to the force. Operating savings would remain at the same real level after 1999; procurement savings would vary depending on the details of weapons acquisition schedules. Added procurement costs for the new lift, pre-positioning, and other initiatives would remain constant from 1996 to 2005, though the operating costs associated with the added lift would increase over the period and reach slightly more than $1 billion a year by 2005.

Savings in 1996 and Subsequent Years

The short-term savings in budget authority from the alternative defense posture would be more modest, only about $3 billion in 1996. In nominal dollars, the budget would be $255 billion rather than $258 billion; in constant 1995 dollars, it would be $247 billion rather than $250 billion (see table 2-2).

Two main rationales for the small immediate savings can be offered. First, in order to avoid excessive disruptions to the force, personnel levels would be reduced by about 3 percent to 4 percent a year under the alternative, less than the rate of about 5 percent during the drawdown of the early 1990s. Thus, for the first year or two, cumulative reductions in the size of the force would be modest. The second reason is that, although a number of weapons development and procurement programs would be terminated, improvements in lift and pre-positioning also would begin in 1996. Thus net savings in investment accounts would be modest.

Outlays in 1996 would decline by about $2.5 billion relative to the administration's plan. Instead of nearly $254 billion, as expressed in constant dollars, they would be just over $251 billion (respective levels in nominal terms would be $261 billion and $258 billion).

Savings would begin to increase by 1997. Budget authority would be about $7 billion less than the BUR that year and roughly $13 billion less

Table 2-2. Savings from the Alternative Defense Posture in Fiscal Year 1996
Billions of current dollars

Type of program or unit	Savings
Suggested cuts	
Operating and support costs	
Active Army divisions	1.0
Army National Guard division-equivalents	0.5
Air Force tactical combat wings	0.2
Marine Corps fighter wing-equivalents	0.3
Aircraft carrier groups and air wings	1.0
Minuteman III ICBMs	0.2
Attack submarines	0.25
Trident submarines	0.1
Weapons acquisition	
F-22 program	2.4
V-22 program	0.5
New attack submarine	1.2
Other activities	
DOE nuclear weapons	0.2
Communications consolidation	0.25
Intelligence consolidation and reform	0.5
DOD medicine	0.25
Defense conversion	1.5
Subtotal	10
Suggested increases[a]	
Additional maritime and afloat pre-positioning	−1.5
Air Force pre-positioned munitions, support equipment, fuel	−1.0
Fast sealift	−0.25
747-class aircraft or equivalent	−2.0
KC-10 or equivalent	−0.75
F-15 production	−1.0
CH-46/53 helicopter replacement	−0.5
UN equipment, training (other militaries)	−0.1
Subtotal	−7.00
Overall defense budget	
Total national defense (050)	3[b]

Sources: CBO, "Implications of Additional Reductions in Defense Spending," p. 16; CBO, *Structuring U.S. Forces after the Cold War*, p. 8; CBO, *Reducing the Deficit*, pp. 11–98; CBO, *The START Treaty and Beyond*, p. 140; *Budget of the United States Government, Fiscal Year 1996*, pp. 121–28; Kosiak, "Analysis of the Fiscal Year 1996 Defense Budget Request," p. 17 and table 10; and General Accounting Office, "Military Afloat Prepositioning," p. 8.

a. Procurement costs for most systems are based on an assumed production profile of ten years. Additional operating costs do not appear in 1996, when no new systems will yet have been built, but do appear at roughly half their steady-state value in 1999 (see table 2-1).

b. The Clinton request for 1996 is $258 billion for the 050 account; the alternative would cost $255 billion (in current dollars).

in 1998. Outlay savings would lag slightly, reaching roughly $6 billion in 1997 and about $12 billion in 1998.

Savings in the Next Decade

The proposed alternative would save even more money than the administration's plan in the next decade. Net savings would remain at about $20 billion from 2000 through 2005. But after 2005, the investments in lift and pre-positioning required by the alternative strategy would be completed and the $8 billion a year allotted for them would no longer be required. Actual savings could prove to be even greater, relatively speaking, if the administration plan's next-generation weapons systems incur the types of cost increases often associated with new weapons systems. My alternative would entail fewer such systems and thus would be less vulnerable to possible increases in their costs.

Even though the specific procurement cuts shown in tables 2-1 and 2-2 will not necessarily apply after 2005, their broad magnitude is consistent with the permanent savings that would be expected from a smaller force. The major systems to be procured in smaller amounts under the alternative force posture are attack and missile submarines, tactical combat aircraft of the Air Force and Navy and Marines, aircraft carrier battle groups, and ground force units. Typical costs for each will be roughly $1.5 billion for submarines, $35 million to $100 million for aircraft, about $10 billion for the ships making up an aircraft carrier battle group, and about $5 billion for the major combat equipment of a heavy division. Associated procurement costs for parts, munitions, and the like for these units will add nearly again as much in costs.[7] Roughly speaking, therefore, thirty fewer submarines would save $45 billion, nine fewer wings of tactical combat aircraft $40 billion to $50 billion, four fewer carrier battle groups about $40 billion, and one less heavy division about $5 billion. The sum of those savings is about $135 billion, which when spread over a weapons lifetime of twenty-five to thirty years yields a net annual savings of about $5 billion. Cuts in associated equipment would take this figure close to $10 billion in the steady state, equal to the amount of procurement cuts that the alternative would produce in 1999.

These numbers can be validated in yet another way. In the thirty years between 1970 and 1999—roughly a full weapons-system life cycle—investment accounts on average represent about 38 percent of DOD's budget, with operations and support accounting for the rest. (The totals

Figure 2-1. Budget Implications of the Clinton Administration's Plan for National Defense, Fiscal Years 1993–2010
Billions of 1995 dollars

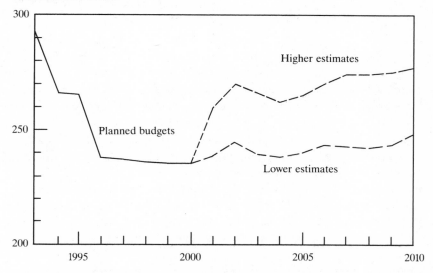

Source: Congressional Budget Office, "An Analysis of the Administration's Future Years Defense Program for 1995 through 1999," CBO Paper (January 1995), p. 50.

for the years 1996 through 1999 are based on the administration's projections). That is, the sum total of procurement; research, development, testing, and evaluation (RDT&E); and military construction has been about two-fifths of all spending—although it ranged from about 35 percent in most of the 1970s and 1990s to 47 percent during the Reagan buildup—and personnel, operations and maintenance, and family housing account for the remaining three-fifths.[8] Thus the proposed alternative's reduction in annual operating and support costs of slightly more than $15 billion should imply a permanent reduction in weapons acquisition costs of about $10 billion.

Such savings could be even more important than they may appear because the BUR force will cost more in the next decade than its projected level of $239 billion in 1999. CBO calculations show that DOD budgets will have to rise by at least $7 billion a year after 1999, primarily because of weapons purchases (see figure 2-1).[9] A more simple-minded calculation that holds operating expenses steady while returning acquisition budgets to their traditional 38 percent share of the overall defense budget suggests that procurement budgets would have to increase by about $10 billion a year, if RDT&E were held constant. DOD's own long-term budget plans confirm this assessment. Real budgets are projected to increase by a total of 2.3 percent, or about $6 billion, from 1999 to 2001, with procurement budgets increasing by $9 billion a year by 2001. Whichever way one calculates, the administration's plan seems likely to cost about $250 billion a year in the next decade, as measured in 1995 dollars. The proposed alternative would also require real budgets to increase somewhat in the early years of the next decade, perhaps to $225 billion a year or somewhat more. But after 2006 budgets could again be allowed to decline to perhaps $220 billion.

Savings under the proposed alternative could prove even greater. As a consequence of weapons systems such as the F-22, V-22, JAST, and F/A-18E/F aircraft, the administration plan could cost more than expected—perhaps as much as $270 billion a year by the end of the next decade (in constant 1995 dollars).[10] Because the proposed alternative would eliminate the first two of those programs, as well as the Centurion new attack submarine, it would be less likely to experience large increases in costs.

As substantial as these cuts may seem, they would provide only about half of defense's "fair share" contribution toward balancing the overall federal budget by 2002—if all programs excluding interest are assumed to take equal reductions of nearly 15 percent. The alternative proposal would result in defense budget and spending levels of $220 billion to $225 billion, as measured in 1995 dollars, in contrast to a level of about $200 billion that would represent defense's "fair share." (Defense budgets would have to descend to well below $200 billion annually if social security were kept entirely off the budget-cutting table.)[11] Many now believe defense will remain off that deficit reduction block and remain at 80 percent of its average cold war budgeting level. But they do so in the face of basic structural factors—the lack of a strategic rival to the United States, the outstanding quality of today's U.S. armed forces, and the strength of the Western alliance—that suggest otherwise.

Notes

1. John Lewis Gaddis, *Strategies of Containment* (New York: Oxford University Press, 1982), p. 30. The five centers are Japan, the United Kingdom, Western Europe, the then Soviet Union, and the United States.

2. For a similar view, see Richard K. Betts, *Military Readiness: Concepts, Choices, Consequences* (Brookings, 1995), pp. 205–07.

3. See "Owens: Get Smart Weapons," *Navy News and Undersea Technology*, October 3, 1994, p. 1.

4. For such an argument, see John D. Steinbruner, "Reluctant Strategic Realignment: The Need for a New View of National Security," *Brookings Review*, vol. 13 (Winter 1995), pp. 4–9.

5. Barry M. Blechman and others, *Key West Revisited: Roles and Missions of the US Armed Forces in the Twenty-First Century* (Washington: Henry L. Stimson Center, March 1993), p. 32; Chairman Les Aspin, House Armed Services Committee, "An Approach to Sizing American Conventional Forces for the Post-Soviet Era," February 25, 1992, chart VII; and William W. Kaufmann and John D. Steinbruner, *Decisions for Defense: Prospects for a New Order* (Brookings, 1991), pp. 65, 73.

6. The precise level of outlays in 1999 would be a function of how cuts in procurement budgets had been made in preceding years, as well as in the cuts for that year indicated in table 2-1. Overall, outlay savings lag savings in spending authority by roughly two years. In a recent year, for example, procurement accounts typically spent 15 percent of their money in the first year (that is, the year for which authority to spend was provided), 31 percent the following year, 27 percent the third year, 13 percent the fourth, and 7 percent the fifth. There was essentially no lag in personnel accounts, and only a modest amount in operations and maintenance accounts: personnel accounts spent 98 percent in the first year and 1 percent in the second; operations and maintenance accounts, 73 percent the first year, then 21 percent and 3 percent in the next two years. But research, development, and testing accounts spent 46 percent the first year, then 40 percent, 8 percent, and 2 percent; military construction, 13, 36, 26, 10, 8, and 3 percent over the first six years; and family housing, 46, 30, 13, 4, 2, and 1 percent. See Joshua M. Epstein, *The 1987 Defense Budget* (Brookings, 1986), p. 5.

For the alternative plan, net budget reductions in the 1996–99 period are due almost entirely to reductions in operations and maintenance accounts, since cuts of about $10 billion in planned acquisition programs are nearly balanced by other procurement increases of about $8 billion for each year.

7. Congressional Budget Office, "The Costs of the Administration's Plan for the Navy through the Year 2010," CBO Memorandum (November 1994), pp. 18–19; CBO, "The Costs of the Administration's Plan for the Air Force through the Year 2010," CBO Memorandum (November 1994), p. 19; and the Congressional Budget Office, *Limiting Conventional Arms Exports to the Middle East* (September 1992), p. 83.

8. See, for example, Department of Defense, Office of the Comptroller, *National Defense Budget Estimates for FY 1995* (March 1994), pp. 84–85; William W. Kaufmann, *Assessing the Base Force* (Brookings, 1992), p. 92; and Department of Defense, Office of the Comptroller, "FY 1996 DOD Budget Briefing," February 6, 1995.

9. Congressional Budget Office, "An Analysis of the Administration's Future Years Defense Program for 1995 through 1999," CBO Paper (January 1995), p. 50.

10. Ibid.

11. Congressional Budget Office, *The Economic and Budget Outlook: Fiscal Years 1996–2000* (January 1995), p. 58.

CHAPTER THREE

THE MILITARY CHALLENGE OF REGIONAL WAR

THE CLINTON ADMINISTRATION's bottom-up review force posture, like the Bush administration's base force that preceded it, envisions the possibility of engaging in full-fledged combat operations in two Desert Storm–like wars at once, probably in Southwest Asia and on the Korean peninsula. This two-theater scenario, more than any other, drives current thinking about the proper size and shape of the U.S. military.

Although a half century of cold war history and associated military doctrine call into question the need to prepare for two major and tactically offensive regional wars at once, there is a deterrent logic to a two-war strategy. Events of 1994—in particular, the October Gulf crisis provoked by Iraqi ground units moving near Kuwait at a time when U.S.–North Korean discord over Pyongyang's nuclear program displayed the potential to deteriorate into a serious crisis—provide concrete evidence that nearly simultaneous major regional crises cannot be ruled out.

There are, however, several points on which current strategy can be challenged. To begin, its current shorthand scenario of a standardized major regional contingency (MRC) can obscure the basic reality that most potential conflicts would, at least for the near term, pit the United States against forces considerably less capable than those of Iraq in 1990. Iran and Iraq are at present rather weak and likely to stay that way for quite a while; in addition, North Korean forces appear to be stagnating while those of South Korea improve.[1] By one useful measure of military capability developed by the Analytic Sciences Corporation, Iraq's current capabilities are only about half as great as in 1990. Syria and North Korea have capabilities roughly two-thirds to three-fourths the magnitude of Iraq's in 1990 (see table 3-1).[2]

Moreover, it is difficult to believe that one can rigorously deduce proper force levels for a two-MRC capability given that Pentagon plan-

Table 3-1. Measures of Military Capability for Key Powers[a]

Country	Army ground forces (standardized divisions)	Tactical combat aircraft (standardized wings)
Bahrain	0.1	0.2
Oman	0.1	0.2
Qatar	0.2	0.1
Kuwait	0.2	0.6
UAE	0.4	0.6
Jordan	1.1	0.5
Saudi Arabia	1.7	2.3
Iran	1.9	2.6
Iraq	3.6	2.4
Egypt	3.2	3.2
Syria	4.7	3.5
Israel	4.6	3.7
South Korea	3.3	1.2
North Korea	4.6	2.6
Iraq in 1990	6	3
China	8	6
Russia	37	18
United States	21	31

Sources: Analytic Sciences Corporation, Rosslyn, Va., February 1995; General Merrill A. McPeak, U.S. Air Force, *Presentation to the Commission on Roles and Missions of the Armed Forces* (Department of Defense, September 1994), p. 60; and Congressional Budget Office, "Planning for Defense: Affordability and Capability of the Administration's Program," CBO Memorandum (March 1994), p. 22.

a. Scores are normalized relative to a U.S. heavy division composed of Abrams M1A1 tanks and associated equipment such as Bradley fighting vehicles and MLRS artillery and a tactical fighter wing with F-16 aircraft. They do not account for the state of repair of weapons or the readiness and sustainability of the units that would use them.

ners revised their own requirements for that strategy downward by 10 percent over the brief space of two years. The Bush administration's base force plan of 1992 determined that an active-duty force of 1.6 million people, with 12 ground combat divisions and 26 air wings, would be needed for such a strategy; two years later, the Clinton administration, again with the full approval of the Joint Chiefs of Staff, revised those figures downward by about 150,000 people, 2 Army divisions, and 6 air wings. Under the Clinton plan, weapons modernization programs allegedly would make it possible to carry out the same strategy with smaller forces; but those modernization programs were under way during the development of the base force doctrine and presumably were incorporated in that plan as well.

Most fundamentally, though, the two-MRC framework fails to take sufficient account of how the revolution in airpower and precision-strike technology, together with the specific focus of U.S. security policy on Southwest Asia and Korea, allows more efficient strategies to be considered. In particular, the United States and any allies should not have to plan on suffering an initial defeat before prevailing. Although such an early setback cannot be ruled out entirely, it is quite unlikely, and a well-chosen U.S. military strategy should be able to make it even more unlikely. The desert of Southwest Asia is highly conducive to air strikes against any hostile troop movements, and the terrain of Korea is sufficiently prepared with fortifications and mines that any enemy thrust could be slowed on the ground while being attacked from the air. Expanded pre-positioning of necessary supplies, including precision munitions—together with enough airlift and tankers to deploy substantial amounts of tactical combat aircraft, some light ground forces, and personnel for pre-positioned heavy equipment—should make possible a successful forward defense of the type NATO envisioned in Europe against a far more capable adversary.

Finally, the notion of a generic MRC also seems to ignore the possibility that means other than war—such as regional arms control or export-limitation arrangements—might help contain the potential scale of conflict in theaters such as Southwest Asia. The Defense Planning Guidance leading to the base force, other Bush administration documents, and the Clinton administration's BUR assumed that the strength of a regional foe would approach that of Iraq in 1990.[3] To be cautious, I assume that Iraq or Iran could remilitarize to that extent, but it hardly seems inevitable that they will, as I argue further in chapter 6.[4]

The Nature of Regional Threats

A regional power can be defined as one that, alone or in conjunction with any close allies it may have, can conduct sustained major military operations only in areas contiguous to its own borders. It is thus an indication of the fundamental security of the United States that its defense planning has the luxury of focusing on such limited potential threats to its own territory or to its major industrialized allies.

The United States also has the luxury of planning to win such wars decisively and with low casualties. Such conditions were achieved in the Gulf War even though coalition forces had to fight on the tactical offensive to uproot entrenched Iraqi forces and drive them from Kuwait. There, the overall coalition advantage in major combat equipment, weighted by quality, was roughly 2:1 on the ground and 4:1 in the air.[5] The United States and its coalition allies did not achieve such decisive victory by any fluke. Independent analysts' predictions, while not generally as optimistic as experience later warranted, were in line with what occurred. Those predictions were informed by data from Arab-Israeli wars involving similar equipment and relative troop training levels, as well as weapons performance data culled from decades of analyzing potential NATO–Warsaw Pact scenarios in Europe.[6]

Some Possible Scenarios

Which regional powers merit the scrutiny of U.S. security policymakers? In terms of expenditures, there is only one major military power in the world, the United States. The world's next seven powers include five U.S. allies as well as China and Russia. More likely foes such as Iraq, Iran, and North Korea are another step down, generally in the range of $10 billion a year in military spending (as estimated by conversions of their defense budgets to dollars through use of official exchange rates). Even if one attempts to compensate for the lower cost of those countries' military personnel through a purchasing-power parity spending comparison, they generally have budgets about a factor of 10 below that of the United States.

In terms of personnel levels the United States does have real competition, in particular China, with armed forces roughly twice as large as the U.S. uniformed forces. Russian and Indian forces are comparable in size to those of the United States; Vietnam's, Turkey's, Iran's, Iraq's, and North Korea's are roughly one-half to two-thirds as large. But when a measure of the amount and technological sophistication of weaponry is factored into those calculations, as made possible by a methodology developed by the Analytic Sciences Corporation, the U.S. advantage over any country besides Russia is very substantial. When an effort is also made to account for training, maintenance, logistics, reconnaissance, and intelligence support levels, it is clear that the United States is unrivaled among the world's military powers and overwhelmingly superior to any plausible foe.[7]

The list of major military powers potentially threatening to important U.S. interests has generally been whittled down to three by recent administrations and Pentagon planners. The Defense Planning Guidance of early 1992, which served as an underpinning for the base force as well as the BUR, placed Iran, Iraq, and North Korea—particularly the latter two—on the final list of concerns. Neither the base force nor the BUR went so far as to say that no other countries could pose threats. But in the end, both relied a good deal on scenarios involving those specific countries to justify their planned forces, and they were right to do so.[8]

Most scenarios not including Iran, Iraq, or North Korea that could involve substantial combat entail less than clear U.S. commitments and interests. A major war between India and Pakistan, for example, might not give the United States any more incentive to become militarily involved than did the previous three such wars. Israel seems easily capable of its own defense at present, assuming the durability of secular rule in Egypt and a pro-U.S. regime in Saudi Arabia as well as no major deterioration in relations with Syria. A possible war between Vietnam and Thailand seems unlikely to engage U.S. interests sufficiently or to threaten Thailand enough to cause Americans to consider a return to an area that represents such an unhappy part of their history.

Some scenarios are, however, more ambiguous. A worst-case example might be a Chinese invasion, or perhaps more likely an aggressive blockade, of Taiwan. The United States might well attempt to help Taiwan break any blockade, with the possibility of localized naval clashes that could ultimately present one or more parties with choices about escalation. A war between India and Pakistan could escalate beyond the scale of previous conflicts in that region and involve the threatened or actual use of nuclear weapons against major population centers. The Mideast political and security environment could worsen drastically as a result of the spread of Islamic fundamentalism.

But another point is also important to emphasize: most of those crises or wars might be exacerbated by a unilateral U.S. response. Therefore, an all-out U.S. military engagement on behalf of one party against another, or simply to enforce a cease-fire, is generally less likely than a multilateral response.

Similarly, in most areas of the world, the probability that a second such conflict would break out at a given moment seems unlikely to be a strong function of whether a first was already under way. In other words, potential aggressors seem much less likely to undertake conflicts on the basis of perceived "windows of opportunity" vis-à-vis the United States than on the basis of specific events and politics in their regions. The prospect of intervention by the United States or other outsiders—unlikely under most circumstances in any case—is not the principal deterrent to conflict now.[9]

Outside powers might be likely to intervene in some cases, perhaps if a war escalated to massive attacks against civilians, the use of weapons of mass destruction, or a general threat to regional stability. Otherwise, the threatened U.S. interests would probably prove too small to justify intervention on basic national security or economic grounds. No country outside of Japan, Europe, or North America conducts trade with the United States at a level exceeding 1 percent of U.S. GDP, and most represent less than 0.1 percent of this activity. The only major caveat concerns imported oil, without which the U.S. economy would need to undergo major adjustments and the economies of allies even more fundamental restructuring.[10]

Even in regard to conflict in the Middle East and Korea, the possibility of simultaneous major conflicts strains credulity. If it were a pressing military concern, Defense Secretary William J. Perry would not have made public comments to the effect that fighting two full-scale regional wars at once is implausible, and that in the event of simultaneous conflicts the United States would seek to "contain" them rather than win both in Desert Storm style at once. Nor would the United States delay in finding some way to improve, very quickly, airlift capabilities that probably leave it unable to claim a true two-war capability at present.[11] One partial solution would be to mandate that all U.S. commercial airlines participate in the Civil Reserve Air Fleet—hardly an extreme measure for a matter deemed to be of fundamental importance to national security—since about 59 percent of all commercial passenger aircraft and 28 percent of cargo aircraft are not currently participants.[12] Another partial solution would be to explore CRAF-like arrangements with European airlines as well as Canada and perhaps Japan.

Two-war doctrine notwithstanding, U.S. planners seem to recognize that deterrence depends more on the degree of U.S. political commitment to the security of other countries than on the precise level of U.S. military capability. In light of the post–Desert Storm clarity of U.S. commitment to the security of both South Korea and the Gulf Cooperation Council countries of the Arabian peninsula, it seems implausible that either Saddam Hussein or the new North Korean leadership would again doubt U.S. and world resolve or test it with a military strike.[13] Tyrants may have extreme goals and ruthless tactics. But those who survive as heads of state generally are able to avoid suicidal blunders. Indeed, the text of the bottom-up review—if not the basic premise of that strategy—seems to agree with this logic. It argues that "history suggests that we most often deter the conflicts that we plan for and actually fight the ones we do not anticipate."[14]

In fairness, the same BUR also points out that a single war could prove more challenging than anticipated. It does seem likely that a future regional adversary would, at a minimum, fight differently than did Saddam, perhaps using certain high-leverage capabilities such as mines and ballistic and cruise missiles—or even weapons of mass destruction or terrorist attacks against U.S. citizens—in tandem with a political strategy that sought to pursue some type of compromise settlement.[15] But the effectiveness of such tactics and their ability to tilt the balance of capabilities on the battlefield are open to serious debate. Particularly in the current threat environment (and probable future one), where potential adversaries are considerably weaker than Iraq in 1990, it seems dubious that a future conflict would be even as challenging as the 1991 Gulf War.

The BUR probably has it about right in that regard, in fact. It assumes that the military forces of potential regional aggressors would include 400,000 to 750,000 total armed personnel, 2,000 to 4,000 tanks, 3,000 to 5,000 armored fighting vehicles, 2,000 to 3,000 artillery pieces, 500 to 1,000 combat aircraft, 100 to 200 naval vessels (primarily patrol craft armed with surface-to-surface missiles) and up to 50 submarines, and 100 to 1,000 SCUD-class ballistic missiles (some possibly with nuclear, chemical, or biological warheads). The United States would plan to deploy nearly as much force as in Desert Storm, and a more modern force than in that conflict, consisting of 4 to 5 Army divisions, 4 to 5 Marine expeditionary brigades, 10 Air Force fighter wings, 100 Air Force heavy bombers, 4 to 5 aircraft carrier battle groups, special operations forces, and National Guard enhanced readiness brigades.[16] Such a force should provide a substantial capability against a regional foe.

Two Desert Storms—or Desert Shields?

Instead of effectively preparing for the equivalent of two simultaneous Desert Storms, the military could base an alternative strategy on responding to simultaneous regional crises early, in the style and at the pace of the October 1994 response to Iraqi troop movements but with the larger forces of Desert Shield if necessary. As a matter of prudence, the United States should also retain enough capability to expand one of those Desert Shield deployments into a Desert Storm–like capability, in which, despite initially suffering setbacks, it would prevail quickly and decisively without requiring help from the major industrialized allies.

Under such a planning framework, responsive airpower, together with the rapid deployment of enough ground forces to protect airfields and the key infrastructure by establishing a perimeter against infantry incursions or armored forces surviving air attack, would form the core of a U.S. military response to a crisis. In Korea, U.S. airpower, in conjunction with South Korean land forces and fortified terrain, may well be all that would be needed against the archaic yet large military forces of North Korea—particularly if the only goal was to impede an invasion.[17] In the Persian Gulf, the desert environment and the much reduced land forces of Iraq also give airpower a decisive edge if it is deployed quickly.

Should Iran or Iraq remilitarize, moreover, it is highly likely that it will take them long enough to do so—about a decade—that the North Korean threat will have declined further in the meantime, mitigating concerns over simultaneous large-scale regional conflicts.[18] In addition, the possibility of further allied help might have been enhanced. In an era when the Western alliance is in need of clear new direction, and when the U.S. public and Congress will probably prove unwilling to shoulder the burden of acting as a lone global policeman for very long, the administration nevertheless assumes that the United States should expect to fight any future regional wars without appreciable assistance from its major allies in Europe or Japan. This assumption in the BUR seems at odds with the National Security Strategy, which states flatly that should U.S. forces be deployed for combat operations, "especially on those matters touching directly the interests of our allies, there should be a proportional commitment from them."[19] The major Western allies of the United States are not only among the world's great military powers; they also share many of the interests that seem most likely to lead the United States into military confrontation, such as ensuring access to Persian Gulf oil, preventing weapons proliferation, and more generally promoting a stable international order.

Given the state of joint Western force planning and decisionmaking today, the authors of the BUR were in one sense appropriately cautious and conservative. Mechanisms to deploy sizable multilateral forces promptly, efficiently, and decisively are not in place at present, even though the concepts of combined joint task forces, the rapid-reaction force, and the Eurocorps have been developed. But policymakers should not err so far in the opposite direction that they effectively turn the

United States into the world's policeman without even being conscious they are doing so. Getting away from a two–Desert Storm planning framework and thinking about how to handle regional conflict more efficiently could help avoid that pitfall.

Sizing U.S. Combat Capabilities

How much military force would be required to undertake an approach to regional warfighting patterned on a "two–Desert Shield" framework, but with enough force to transform one of the operations into something more like Desert Storm without handicapping the other?

Force Structure

By the time of its completion at the end of October 1990, the Desert Shield deployment involved some 200,000 U.S. troops, including roughly three Army divisions, a division-sized Marine force and accompanying air support, ten Air Force air wings, and three Navy aircraft carriers.[20] A similar but smaller defensive deployment in October 1994, at the time of Iraqi troop movements that appeared threatening to Kuwait, involved some 50,000 U.S. troops, including about eight wings of aircraft and elements of two ground divisions.[21]

A corps of U.S. forces would be large enough to cover several potential axes of enemy advance. For example, a corps-sized U.S. ground force for the Korean context seems sensible because there are three main potential axes of advance near Seoul in the demilitarized zone, each of which could be defended under this scheme by a U.S. division in addition to South Korean forces and U.S. airpower. In Southwest Asia, the main channels of likely attack into Kuwait or Saudi Arabia along the Persian Gulf are also few in number and involve a corridor about one hundred kilometers wide, all of which can easily be brought within weapons range by two to three U.S. divisions deploying across the corridor.[22] It was such a philosophy that guided the initial Desert Shield defensive deployment and planning for the types of ground force operations that would have been undertaken if Iraq had chosen to attempt attacks against Saudi Arabia by October 1990. Military planners at the time, as well as the authors of official accounts of the war by the Department of Defense and the U.S. Army, believed that such a one-corps deployment together with a strong airpower complement would provide a very reliable defensive capability against the much larger Iraqi forces. (They would also have been aided by a British brigade and about two fighter squadrons, some French light forces, and regional allies.) Indeed, planners seriously considered attacking with a single corps, but ultimately considered the plan somewhat risky and likely to result in moderately high U.S. casualties.[23]

The U.S. military's technological advantages in mobility, sensors, and munitions, which allow tactics based on maneuver and attack behind enemy lines, reduce the importance of maintaining a given so-called force-to-space ratio.[24] But for a defensive holding action across a given-sized front, in which there is little uncertainty about the likely direction or size of any attack, it is reassuring and appropriately conservative to envision a U.S. ground force cordon that would not stretch divisions and corps-level assets out over a greater distance than they are accustomed to operating in.

The two–Desert Shield framework thus suggests a total requirement for U.S. forces of roughly six active divisions and sixteen tactical fighter wings. Army and Marine forces would make up the former category, and Air Force, Marine, and Navy units the latter.

But it would be imprudent, as argued before, to count fully on the success of a moderate-sized rapid-response deployment. One of those missions might wind up having to look more like Desert Storm; it could fit the mold of the large MRC envisioned in the bottom-up review, with some six ground divisions and fifteen tactical fighter wings. In that event, the sum total of a "Desert Shield plus Desert Storm" warfighting requirement would be about nine active division-equivalents of ground combat capability and twenty-three wing-equivalents of tactical combat aircraft.

Keeping at least some Marine or light Army units involved in a particularly sensitive peace operation should be possible, even in the event of simultaneous regional crises involving major U.S. interests. For that reason, it would be desirable to keep an additional active Marine division and an additional active Army light division above and beyond the nine discussed above. It would also be sensible to retain several wings of tactical combat aircraft for operations such as those in Iraq and Bosnia today. Having a slightly larger force would also provide a hedge against a very difficult regional warfighting scenario. Reserve ground forces—particularly the fifteen enhanced readiness brigades supported by the BUR—and potential help from the European allies would represent additional sources of insurance of last resort.

Table 3-2. An Alternative Defense Posture for Major Combat Operations

Type of program or unit	BUR	Alternative
Suggested cuts		
Active Army heavy divisions	5	4
Active Army light divisions	5	4
Army National Guard division-equivalents	14	8
Marine Corps fighter wing-equivalents	5	2
Air Force active combat wings	13	13
Air Force reserve combat wings	7	5
Aircraft carrier battle groups and air wings	12/11	8/7
Navy attack submarines	45–55	35
F-22 fighter	440	0
V-22 aircraft	425	0
DDG-51 destroyer	Buy 16 more	Buy 8 more
Communications	$20 billion/year	$19 billion/year
Intelligence	$28 billion/year	$26 billion/year
Suggested increases		
Marine Corps pre-positioned brigade sets[a]	3	4
Army pre-positioned brigade sets[a]	4	6
Army forward-deployed brigades[a]	3	3
Air Force pre-positioned munitions, support equipment, fuel[a]	Modest	2 weeks' combat supply
Fast sealift capacity	2 divisions	3 divisions
747-class or equivalent airlift	0	100
KC-10 or equivalent tankers	60	120
F-15E fleet	200	400
Marine CH-46/CH-53 helicopters or equivalent	0	375

a. In or near Korea and Southwest Asia.

Thus the alternative force posture suggested here includes eleven active ground combat divisions and twenty-seven wing-equivalents of aircraft. More precisely, it would include eight active-duty Army divisions (one less heavy division and one less light division than in the BUR framework), three active-duty Marine expeditionary forces of division size, and eighteen Air Force tactical fighter wings. As explained below, it would also consist of seven wings of carrier aircraft, and two wing-equivalents of Marine Corps aircraft instead of the five now in the force structure (see table 3-2). By way of contrast, the BUR calls for thirteen active-duty ground combat divisions, including both Marine and Army elements, as well as thirty-six wing-equivalents of tactical combat aircraft.

How does one justify such large cuts in Navy and Marine Corps air capabilities? For the most likely regional conflicts, aircraft carriers would probably not be needed in large numbers because access to airfields on land would be available. But the alternative force posture would retain eight carriers and seven carrier air wings in the force structure just in case. This would be a sufficient number to establish initial air superiority and provide at least localized ground-attack capability in one regional conflict, for the worst-case scenario in which land bases had been destroyed or otherwise rendered inaccessible.

The BUR review concluded that five carriers would be sufficient for a generic regional war. A set of war games run by the Navy and Marine Corps in 1993 found that five to nine carriers would be adequate to help establish a land foothold for a worst-case Southwest Asia scenario in which land bases were not readily available in the early stages of combat.[25] Moreover, with a fleet of roughly eight carriers, seven of which could be deployed fairly quickly, the United States could achieve parity in numbers of tactical aircraft against any likely regional foe (as the Israeli air force did in its dominant air campaigns against Arab adversaries). Numerical parity may be even more than is needed to establish air supremacy, but as a conservative approach it seems a reasonable benchmark. Factoring in quality, it would provide at least a 3:1 overall hardware edge for U.S. pilots in the skies today and at least 2:1 even against a foe that over the next decade acquired a somewhat stronger air force than Iraq had in 1990.[26]

As discussed in chapter 4, eight carriers—roughly four for each "half of the world"—should also provide sufficient flexibility to conduct occasional tours and, when necessary, crisis response of the scale that typically has been employed by the United States. For major crises, a task force of three to four aircraft carriers and escorting vessels, though still small by warfighting standards, would be more capable than any regional power's aggregate air force and thus pose a very substantial deterrent or limited-strike capability.

The need for the Marine Corps to keep its own integrated air force is very dubious. In the Gulf War, many of its aircraft participated in the broader air campaign rather than in close air support and did so in rather mediocre fashion by contrast with generally more advanced and interoperable Air Force systems. By comparison, having the equivalent of just two squadrons of dedicated aircraft per division-equivalent of Marines for close air support, and relying on the Air Force or Navy for air interdiction and strategic strike, might actually improve the coordination of the U.S. air battle.[27] A caveat: this analysis assumes that the Air Force can be convinced to honor Marine requests for air support more effectively than it did, according to some reports, during much of the Gulf War.[28]

Modernization

The above discussion focuses on force structure, and that of the next chapter on the actual day-to-day and month-to-month operations of forces. But weapons modernization policies are also of central importance; some programs are discussed here and others in chapter 4.

A recognition of the tremendous U.S. advantage over regional threats would allow several significant changes in major modernization programs. To begin, use of Los Angeles–class submarines could be extended through a combination of overhauls and new production.[29] These submarines could continue to constitute the core of the fleet, with ten Seawolfs constituting a "silver torpedo" force that would assure that overall U.S. submarine capability would be second to none. Such a fleet would provide a decisive numerical and qualitative edge against two regional foes at once, each of which will have at most a few operational and modern submarines of its own (Iran now has two, Iraq and North Korea none).[30]

In tactical combat aircraft realms, the F-22 advanced tactical fighter could be canceled. Although the Eurofighter, Rafale, and advanced Russian programs could put improved aircraft into the hands of certain potential adversaries in the future, they are unlikely to exceed the capabilities of the F-15.[31] Even in cases where a regional adversary might obtain some next-generation aircraft, the chances are negligible that it could ever attain levels of target acquisition, command and control, munitions performance, and pilot training to rival the United States.

The real balance of importance seems likely to be U.S. attack aircraft capability versus the air defenses of potential regional adversaries, given that it is through airpower that the United States hopes to destroy much of the armor of any future foe. The F-22 would do little on that score. It would seem to make more sense for the United States to continue pursuing a modernized multipurpose aircraft for late in the next decade and to purchase more of the world-class F-15 aircraft in the interim than to add billions of dollars of insurance to its air superiority margin now.

Particularly in light of its ambitious programs to expand and improve a wide variety of precision munitions to be launched from land, sea, and air-based systems, focusing near-term attention on platforms is a low priority. The joint advanced strike program will incorporate stealth in more modest—and yet substantially more economical—degrees.[32] (See table 3-3 for a summary of current modernization programs for munitions.)

Logistics and Pre-positioning

The question of how much force is no more important than the question of how quickly that force can be deployed in a major crisis. Throughout the 1990s, in fact, top military leaders have identified potential shortfalls in lift as the most likely handicap to a successful waging of two simultaneous regional wars.[33] Accordingly, the recent update to the Pentagon's mobility requirements study reportedly argues that any problems U.S. forces might encounter in regional conflict would be during the initial "halting" phase of the operation, when fewer U.S. forces were available for combat.[34]

Likely Warning Time

U.S. intelligence reportedly expects to have five to seventeen days of clear military warning of a major attack by a regional foe.[35] Because it could take U.S. intelligence several days to figure out that an enemy mobilization was under way, the implication is that a foe would need at least ten days and perhaps three weeks to prepare a major assault.[36]

Less warning might be afforded for more limited enemy maneuvers, however, such as the several brigades of Iraqi forces that threatened Kuwait in October 1994. For this reason, today's stationing of roughly a wing and a half of combat aircraft and at least one brigade of U.S. forces in Southwest Asia represents a desirable development. An ability to reinforce within several days is also needed; in other words, it is not only necessary to complete a full Desert Shield–like deployment within ten days from its inception, it is also important to make some of that deployment within, say, five days. Munitions and fuel for the aircraft must be available in that time period too, meaning that they must be pre-positioned at least partly on land or in the immediate littoral of the country to be defended.

Table 3-3. Acquisition Schedules for Next-Generation Precision Munitions, Fiscal Years 1995–99

Costs in millions of dollars of budget authority

Weapons system	1995[a]	1996	1997	1998	1999	Five-year total
Army						
Brilliant antiarmor submunition						
Quantity	0	0	0	547	882	1,429
Procurement costs	0	0	0	128	139	267
Total costs	119	194	187	331	252	1,083
Javelin advanced antitank weapons system-medium						
Quantity	374	858	942	859	1,156	4,189
Procurement costs	131	172	169	160	154	785
Total costs	162	172	169	160	154	816
Laser Hellfire						
Quantity	830	0	0	0	0	830
Procurement costs	80	0	0	0	0	80
Total costs	80	0	0	0	0	80
Longbow Hellfire						
Quantity	0	364	1,050	1,400	1,525	4,339
Procurement costs	42	198	264	282	304	1,090
Total costs	78	198	264	282	304	1,125
Sense-and-destroy-armor						
Quantity	0	0	264	348	492	1,104
Procurement costs	0	0	115	112	130	357
Total costs	72	88	162	159	186	668

Less warning also might be available for a fairly large North Korean attack on South Korea. However, that concern is mitigated by the U.S. force structure in the region: two Army brigades and a wing of tactical combat aircraft in South Korea, a second aircraft force with roughly four squadrons of combat planes in Japan, and generally another wing aboard a nearby aircraft carrier.[37] Clinton administration pre-positioning initiatives are also adding substantial ready-reaction capability. They include modernizing deployed tanks and adding another half-division's complement of tanks to storage; adding about one hundred Bradley fighting vehicles, twenty-four Apache attack helicopters, and a battalion of Patriot antimissile defenses; and beefing up logistics units.[38] Permanently stationing one or two joint surveillance and target attack radar system (joint STARS) aircraft in Korea, once a few more aircraft are built, also might be a wise addition, as would pre-positioned precision munitions. With those additions, the potential for a short-warning-time attack would be

Table 3-3 *(continued)*

Weapons system	1995[a]	1996	1997	1998	1999	Five-year total
Navy						
Amraam Aim-120A						
Quantity	106	180	306	303	278	1,173
Procurement costs	85	129	203	201	197	815
Total costs	113	174	258	251	254	1,048
Javelin advanced antitank weapon system-medium						
Quantity	0	129	265	601	790	1,785
Procurement costs	0	5	15	35	57	112
Total costs	0	29	44	100	102	275
Rolling airframe missile weapon system						
Quantity	240	240	240	215	0	935
Procurement costs	65	75	75	67	63	345
Total costs	84	103	100	87	72	445
Air Force						
Amraam-Aim (includes Seek Eagle costs)						
Quantity	412	460	338	373	282	1,865
Procurement costs	317	314	261	304	244	1,439
Total costs	388	368	313	331	288	1,688
Sensor-fused weapon						
Quantity	260	526	970	1,204	1,134	4,094
Procurement costs	109	173	271	299	278	1,130
Total costs	111	174	273	301	280	1,138
Joint service						
Joint direct-attack munition (JDAM)						
Quantity	0	0	0	310	355	665
Procurement costs	0	0	0	109	121	230
Total costs	110	145	149	200	184	787
Joint standoff weapon (JSOW)						
Quantity	0	0	300	387	500	1,187
Procurement costs	0	26	133	138	154	451
Total costs	79	79	178	151	154	640
Total costs[b]	1,396	1,724	2,097	2,353	1,892	9,793

Source: Congressional Budget Office. "Selected Weapons Costs from the President's 1995 Program" (May 1994).

a. The 1995 requests have since been acted on by Congress; those for 1996 and beyond have been modified in some cases in the president's budget request for 1996.

b. Totals include research. development. test and evaluation funds as well as those for military construction in some cases.

largely addressed since the United States would have nearly half of a Desert Shield capability already based in theater.

Indeed, applying the Desert Shield requirement to the Korean setting is quite cautious and conservative. Given the strength of South Korean ground forces and the degree to which roads, bridges, and other infrastructure have been preconfigured with explosives that could be detonated at the first sign of attack, U.S. forces currently deployed in theater would probably be all the help South Korea would require to halt an invasion. U.S. air reinforcements alone would make that defense extremely robust and provide at least some types of offensive capability to the South Korean and U.S. coalition forces.[39]

A longer warning of a more ambiguous sort is likely before any regional conflict, since any attack would probably occur during a serious political crisis. Such political warning generally should not be counted on for military purposes, however. As Richard Betts observed, most wars grow out of political crises, yet still wind up beginning in surprise attacks by one side. This is sometimes due to the negligence of the other side's leaders, but often because of their worry that their own military preparation might be escalatory and therefore more dangerous than remaining vulnerable to sudden enemy attack.[40]

Response to a Crisis

A U.S. force that completes a one-corps, eight-wing deployment within ten days to two weeks is highly likely to be capable of sustaining a robust defense with low casualties to itself and high attrition to an advancing regional foe. A response capability along these lines is analogous to the standard that the United States set for itself in the context of a NATO war in Europe, where it planned to have six divisions and roughly twenty wing-equivalents deployed within ten days of the beginning of a crisis.[41]

Such a U.S. response to a major regional crisis would look something like this: tankers would support tactical combat aircraft and airlift flying directly to the theater of concern. Airlift would deploy helicopters, command and control assets, Patriot missile defense systems, two to three brigades of airborne or other light forces (such as the 82d Airborne Division or Rangers), and other personnel to man pre-positioned equipment as well as the assets being flown over. Ground forces would then provide security at airfields and ports, particularly important in South-

Table 3-4. Chronology of a Rapid Crisis Response to Southwest Asia under the Alternative Defense Posture

Type of U.S. unit[a]	Arrival time (days after decision to deploy)[b]	Requisite number of flights	
		C-141[c]	KC-10[c]
Wings 2 through 5 of tactical aircraft and support	2–4	200	100
Brigade 2 of heavy forces to join land-based pre-positioned equipment[d]	2–4	300	75
Brigades 1 and 2 of airborne/light forces	2-4	500	125
Wings 6 through 8 of tactical aircraft	5–7	150	75
Brigade 3 of heavy forces to join pre-positioned equipment[d]	5–7	300	75
Brigade 3 of airborne/light forces	5–7	250	65
Marine brigade 1 to join MPS ship-based equipment	5–7	300	75
Marine brigade 2	8–10	300	75
Brigade 4 of heavy forces to join pre-positioned equipment[d]	8–10	300	75
Additional munitions, parts, support for tactical aircraft	8–10	200	50
AWACS, JSTARS, Patriot	8–10	Less than 100	Less than 25
Other general support	8–10	100	25
Tanker support for bombers, combat aircraft	8–10	0	50

a. The numbers reflect a running total of units deployed and do not correspond to the actual numerical designations of specific units (for example, 82d Airborne Division). The arrival times of aircraft are staggered to account for the limited capacity of bases in the theater of destination; equipment arriving in days 2 through 4 represents the first sortie of aircraft from the United States (or other bases of origin), that arriving in days 5 through 7 the second, and that arriving in days 8 through 10 the third. One wing of tactical aircraft and one brigade of heavy forces are assumed to already be in place.

b. Deploying a given size force to Korea would probably take slightly less time due to the larger peacetime deployment of U.S. forces in Korea and the reliability of access to refueling bases in Alaska and Hawaii.

c. Or the equivalent in other types of aircraft. Under the alternative force posture, the total capacity of the fleets would be roughly 1,200 C-141 equivalents and 300 KC-10 equivalents. Of the refueling aircraft, roughly 120 KC-10 equivalents—that is, the KC-10s themselves—could be used instead as lift, and in that capacity would represent another 200 C-141 equivalents. To account for the inevitable inefficiencies in loading and unloading equipment, however, it is assumed in these calculations that only about 80 percent of the total airlift capacity of the fleet would be profitable employed.

d. Heavy forces include major ground combat equipment, helicopters, personnel, and support equipment.

west Asia, where the initial U.S. presence would be quite modest. Tankers would also support these lift operations as well as some initial combat missions by bombers or tactical aircraft (see table 3-4).

Maritime pre-positioning vessels would set sail for ports within a day of the outbreak of a major crisis and arrive within roughly five to seven days, if based on Guam or Diego Garcia and headed respectively to

Korea or the Persian Gulf. As they arrived, their personnel would be arriving to meet them; unloading and redeployment of equipment on ships would take another five days to a week, which means that those pre-positioned forces would be deployed for combat within about two weeks of the outbreak of a crisis.[42] Finally, an additional heavy Army division could arrive by fast sealift some twenty to twenty-five days after the crisis began, reinforcing the corps-sized deployment and replacing some or all of the light infantry forces, if desired.

Further Improvements in Logistics and Pre-positioning

The United States now has eight fast sealift roll-on roll-off SL-7 ships, capable of carrying roughly one division's worth of equipment (the equivalent of about 200,000 tons of combat equipment, which can be carried on roughly 1.25 million square feet of cargo space).[43] It is adding greater amounts, roughly 2 million to 2.5 million square feet, of medium-speed lift and pre-positioned lift.[44] The military also has Marine pre-positioning capabilities of roughly the equivalent of one division, divided into three squadrons at Diego Garcia in the Indian Ocean, Guam and Saipan in the western Pacific, and the western Atlantic Ocean. In addition to forces permanently stationed in Korea, Japan, and Southwest Asia and maritime pre-positioning ships already based nearby, it is adding two pre-positioned Army brigade sets ashore in the Southwest Asia region as well as a land-based Army brigade set ashore in Korea and another Army brigade set afloat between the two theaters.[45]

Under the alternative force posture suggested here, the United States would buttress its rapid deployment and pre-positioning policies further. Pre-positioning would be improved particularly in Southwest Asia, where the United States has only a very modest ground force presence and relatively weak regional allies. Two brigades' worth of heavy equipment for the Southwest Asian theater in addition to what the administration plans would be deployed overseas, no further away than Diego Garcia. This approach would raise the overall level of U.S. pre-positioning in the area to two division-equivalents. One brigade set would come from the current Marine pre-positioning in Norway. Another would come from Army surplus in Europe or from other stocks in the United States. But it is important that the equipment be capable: it is the targeting and accurate fire capabilities of U.S. ground equipment that did so much to establish overwhelming U.S. advantages in the Gulf War.[46] Such advantages are particularly important in the early stage of conflict, when overall U.S. force levels in the theater of combat would be rather modest.

In regard to Korea, strong South Korean forces and the 2d U.S. Infantry Division already provide a substantial capability to defend key axes of attack and hold ports and airfields. However, it would be useful to buttress that capability; the United States is already adding one Army brigade set, and with a second the Army would have two brigades deployed and two pre-positioned in that theater. In addition to those Army sets and the maritime pre-positioning ships (MPS) based near Guam and Saipan, the MPS squadron based near Florida could also be located to that area (either to the same Guam-Saipan region or Okinawa). With such an approach, the military would also have two full division-equivalents of ground force capability—roughly four Army brigades and two Marine brigades—deployed or pre-positioned in Korea just as it would in Southwest Asia.

The need for pre-positioning is not limited to ground force equipment. About half of the roughly 35,000 tons of ordnance dropped from aircraft during the Gulf War came from pre-positioned stocks. It consisted primarily of less advanced munitions; advanced models were not pre-deployed for security reasons. (Recall that no substantial U.S. ground forces were then in place to monitor and protect them.) Pre-positioned fuel and equipment were also important; together with munitions, materials stored in Southwest Asia before the Gulf War valued about $1 billion and would have needed some 10,000 airlift missions had they required transportation from the United States.[47]

For future purposes, it would be prudent to pre-position substantial stocks of precision ordnance in both Southwest Asia and Korea, enough to carry out the type of two-week-long campaign discussed below. That might imply up to 15,000 precision munitions, or roughly the number used in the entire Gulf War, for each theater. Assuming an average cost for advanced munitions of $100,000, as with current ordnance, means that the value of munitions pre-positioning in each theater would be about $1.5 billion, and an average cost to operate each of the ships holding whatever portion of those stocks was kept at sea might be $50 million a year.[48] With a mix of current-generation and next-generation munitions such as the brilliant antiarmor submunition (costing $150,000 to $200,000 per complete weapon), costs per theater might be about $2 billion.[49] In addition to improving the responsiveness of U.S. military forces, extra stocks of such munitions would provide a welcome cushion if a war actually occurred and drained some of the U.S. stockpile.

The United States would also, as noted, purchase another division-equivalent of fast sealift under the proposal advanced here. One-time costs associated with all these logistics initiatives would total about $5 billion, and annual operating costs would be several hundred million dollars.[50]

The Navy's fuel tanker ships should also be modernized, more or less across the board, in light of their current poor condition yet absolutely central importance for rapid force deployability and sustainability. Thus a fleet of some ten dedicated ships would be retained despite current plans to rely more on the commercial market.[51]

In addition, pre-positioning of fuel is important and should be augmented. During the peak of the Gulf War, some 15 million gallons of jet fuel, or roughly 50,000 tons, was consumed daily by the Air Force alone (over the course of the war, coalition forces consumed about $2 billion of fuel, or roughly 2 billion gallons).[52] Using the standard that comparable amounts of fuel per aircraft should be available for daily use for two weeks of an airpower-based war, U.S. forces should have 500,000 tons of jet fuel alone pre-positioned. Making sure that aircraft would have this amount might lead roughly to a doubling of the amount of pre-positioned jet fuel that was available in Desert Shield and Desert Storm. Were most of it based at sea, a single large ship might suffice to carry the added amount for each theater. The cost would be roughly $100 million in fuel, a comparable amount for the ship, and roughly $50 million a year in operating costs for the ship.[53] Comparable amounts of money could provide additional fuel for the early days of ground operations.

Deploying roughly eight wings of aircraft (about 700 planes) and deploying personnel to rejoin pre-positioned equipment on land or ships could be done, at current levels of lift, in roughly two weeks for a single region, even under conservative assumptions about access to bases for refueling and unloading.[54] This deployment would benefit from about 50 million ton-miles per day of airlift equivalent, consisting of some 240 C-141 aircraft, 125 C-5 aircraft, and about 310 airliners—half cargo and half passenger—in the Civil Reserve Air Fleet (CRAF). It would also involve some 550 KC-135 aircraft and 60 KC-10 tanker-transport aircraft. If intratheater transport was also required, the more than 500 C-130 aircraft in the U.S. inventory would shuttle equipment and people from site to site.[55]

The alternative force posture suggested here would expand those capabilities substantially, making possible deployment of a Desert Shield–like force to a single theater within about ten days (table 3-4). It would achieve and sustain an airlift capacity of some 70 million ton-miles per day by early in the next century, slightly above the official goal of 66 million ton-miles per day of the 1980s. It might acquire that capacity by adding 100 747-class aircraft to its fleet while also either completing procurement of the full 120 C-17 fleet or reopening the C-5 line.[56] (If half of the additional KC-10 tankers recommended below were also counted as airlift, consistent with DOD's standard approach, the capacity would reach 75 million ton-miles per day.)

A capability of 70 million ton-miles per day would translate into a sustainable delivery rate of some 10,000 tons per day for a deployment to the Persian Gulf or Korea (each of which is about 7,000 miles from an average shipping point in the United States). This capacity represents an average of nearly 400 C-141 sorties per day or the equivalent. (However, unless this capacity is used efficiently, actual performance might be substantially less, as it was in the Gulf War, where peak airlift rates were only about 20 million ton-miles per day, or half the theoretical capacity of the fleet.) The purchase of 747-class transport aircraft would entail costs of about $25 billion above current plans over the next decade and $500 million a year in operating costs thereafter.[57]

In addition, it would be essential to ensure the adequacy of the tanker refueling fleet. Nearly half of the KC-135 fleet, or 262 aircraft out of 629, and 46 of 60 KC-10s were used in the Gulf War for refueling purposes.[58] In order to meet my ten-day requirement for a Desert Storm–like force, however, a modest expansion of the U.S. tanker fleet is called for, particularly in light of the pending retirement of some KC-135 aircraft, which will reduce the capacity of the fleet by roughly 10 percent.[59] By doubling the KC-10 fleet to 120 planes, U.S. refueling capacity would be expanded by more than one quarter.[60] The costs associated with doing so would be about $5 billion, spent over a decade, and then annual operating costs of about $300 million a year.

What can be deployed with a daily rate of nearly 400 C-141 deliveries, or, to be more conservative and account for imperfect scheduling and base use, roughly 300 deliveries? Deploying a light or airmobile division requires roughly 300 to 400 C-141 sorties or the equivalent with a mix of aircraft, and an airborne division with support equipment requires some 800 sorties.[61] Getting support equipment for eight wings of tactical combat aircraft into place could entail about 300 to 400 C-141 sorties (though ideally some should be pre-positioned, reducing the airlift requirement).[62] Deploying those assets of a heavy brigade that cannot readily be stored on pre-positioning ships, such as helicopters, could entail about 100 sorties of C-141 aircraft. Finally, deploying a contingent of 50,000 people—roughly 10,000 tons, if allowances are made for some basic supplies—would entail about 400 sorties as well, though it would be unlikely to rely on military aircraft and instead would use the Civil Reserve Air Fleet.

With such enhanced capabilities, within ten days the United States could deploy a light division, AWACS and joint STARS aircraft, Patriot batteries, round-out equipment for heavy forces, and roughly 75,000 personnel for the heavy forces and the Marine forces that had pre-positioned equipment.[63] Simultaneous regional crises could thus be handled effectively if separated by ten days or more, a closer spacing than assumed in the bottom-up review.

What could go wrong with the above plan? For one thing, bases might be a constraint. According to the Military Traffic Management Command of the U.S. Transportation Command, ports and airfields are more than ample for current deployment plans in both Korea and Southwest Asia. But air traffic in Saudi Arabia in the early period of Desert Shield was limited to about seventy aircraft a day, and the above strategy would require up to four times that.[64] Thus airfield improvements in the countries of destination would be needed, and the alternative budget would provide several hundred million dollars for such purposes over the course of the next three years. In addition, retaining firm commitments from European allies to supply base access for any major U.S. military involvement in the region, as was provided in the Gulf War, is a minimum short-term goal of any reasonable burden-sharing arrangement.[65] Over the medium term, the European allies must better configure their forces and improve their lift to help with large regional warfighting operations for common Western concerns such as Gulf stability (see chapter 6).

Finally, there would be requirements for some of the accessories of lift that are difficult to identify entirely in an unclassified force planning document but that are every bit as critical to a smooth operation as the planes and ships containing supplies. These include cranes for unloading equipment on shore or ship; fuel bladders, hydrant systems, and refueling vehicles; air traffic controllers; and pilots and repair crews. Some of these types of resources were severely taxed in Desert Storm, with 90 percent of the Air Force's assets being deployed to the Gulf theater. Expansions in such mundane, relatively inexpensive, and yet essential systems, if not already in progress, should be undertaken.[66]

Marine Corps amphibious assault capability is unlikely to be called upon as it was at Inchon, but it proved itself in the Gulf War as a useful strategic device nonetheless. War games and other considerations suggest that the currently programmed capability of 2.5 Marine expeditionary brigades should be adequate, when working in tandem with Navy air, to establish a foothold even where none is immediately available.

Understanding Regional Military Campaigns

What if the one-corps, eight-wing model resembling Desert Shield, yet employing greater amounts of pre-positioning, airlift and tanker capabilities, and precision-attack aircraft, were not successful in deterring an adversary? In such an event, the U.S. force in conjunction with allies would need to defeat the advancing enemy quickly and decisively. In the aftermath of Arab-Israeli wars, the 1991 Gulf War, and other sources of military information and experience, a number of broad judgments about the probable course of such a conflict can be formed.

Qualitative Considerations

Not only U.S. air superiority but U.S. air supremacy, defined as denying the adversary any meaningful use of aircraft throughout the theater of conflict, can be reliably achieved against a foe like North Korea or Iraq.[67] In addition, U.S. countermeasures against ground-based air defenses, combined with the ability to deliver an overwhelming attack against most major fixed sites such as air-defense radars, mean that the United States and allies could count on using the airspace in a theater of battle to their great advantage (though not without at least some attrition to aircraft from air defense weapons operating individually). They could loiter to search for tanks, artillery, and hardened shelters for aircraft and other assets, and then deliver precision-guided munitions against those targets.[68]

The capability to conduct such attacks at any given time could be constrained by severe weather, but it is questionable how much an adversary could exploit such circumstances. It would be hard pressed to build a reliance on foul conditions into a battle plan that would have to begin preparations a number of days before attacking. Moreover, as in Desert Storm, U.S. ground forces would have tremendous advantages over adversarial units even if close-air support was temporarily disrupted by weather, as was the case during much of the ground war in Operation Desert Storm.[69]

Because of joint STARS aircraft—as well as infrared sensors and laser range finders on ground combat vehicles and extremely proficient crews—the United States could also expect to enjoy overwhelming advantages in ground combat. This advantage would be particularly great against adversaries armed primarily with T-55 and T-62 genre technology, but even against more modern Soviet equipment. In fact, in the Gulf War several M1A1 Abrams tanks were hit by T-72 rounds but not damaged; over the course of the entire war, U.S. tank reliability rates were over 90 percent and fewer than 10 Abrams were damaged by enemy fire. In general, U.S. units would see an adversary's forces well before being detected themselves and would be able to fire from such distances with good prospects of destroying an enemy platform on the first shot. Such asymmetries produced ground-combat exchange ratios of more than 100 to 1 in the U.S. favor in the Gulf War. Although such ratios may have been partly a function of a dispirited and unusually disorganized Iraqi force, as well as ideal conditions and an excellent battle plan for the United States, certainly combat exchange ratios above 10:1 could be expected in the future.[70]

Unfortunately, particularly in Korea, enemy forces might be able to cause substantial damage to various civilian assets during an attack. Such damage is difficult to preclude with any set of tactics, including preemptive strike. Fortunately, enemy forces would make themselves vulnerable to counterartillery tracking, and then both artillery and air assault, whenever they fired. In addition, their ability to damage U.S. military assets would be limited since they would generally not be able to locate or accurately attack mobile targets.

Simple "Dynamic" Calculations

With such basic considerations in hand, it is possible to turn to simple mathematics to explain, and test, the concept of a Desert Shield–like strategy for responding to regional crises. (See appendix A for a discussion of other popular mathematical tools in defense analysis.) One hopes that in places where U.S. lives are on the line, and the clarity of U.S. commitments has been proven by past wars, reinforcements of permanent U.S. forces would suffice to deter encroachment by a potential adversary. But ultimately, such a deterrent should not be depended on exclusively and could not be expected to be strong unless it reflected a real warfighting capability on the part of the forces deployed. Thinking through the timing of a military engagement and getting a rough feeling for the pace at which events could occur are important ways to assess that capability.

Consider the way a campaign would unfold. First, an adversary would need to mobilize and otherwise prepare for war: such activities, if conducted on a theaterwide scale, would be difficult for U.S. intelligence to miss. Such early indicators should provide at least five days to a week for U.S. forces, together with those of regional allies, to reinforce forward positions and heighten alert levels.

Once a U.S. adversary attacked, in either Korea or Southwest Asia, it would be very hard pressed to advance more than a few kilometers a day. During the North Korean offensive of 1950, attacks against a disorganized South Korean force were able to achieve advances of fifteen kilometers a day. But movements on the order of three to five kilometers would be ambitious for a force possessing no more than parity in overall ground capability (nothing near the 3:1 or 5:1 effective combat ratios generally enjoyed by rapidly advancing armies in World War II) and facing overwhelming disadvantages in the air as well as terrain prepared with various obstacles and explosives.[71] Thus, though there would be important differences in the two theaters, the likely scenario for a conflict in either Southwest Asia or Korea would entail at least one week's time for an enemy to move the distance that it would have to traverse in order to reach fixed U.S. and allied assets.

During that week of combat, U.S. ground forces that included at least 500 tanks and similar amounts of artillery and armored personnel carriers could themselves fire tens of thousands of rounds with the potential to destroy a ten-division adversarial force (containing roughly 10,000 major combat vehicles and a total of perhaps 20,000 vehicles). But in all likelihood, they would have substantial help from air assets, which under good conditions could accomplish the lion's share of the work. With roughly four wings of attack aircraft (numbering 300 planes) and roughly as many helicopters together flying 1,000 sorties a day, some 5,000 precision munitions a day could be fired and at least 1,000 enemy armored vehicles destroyed (see table 3-5).[72]

As discussed in appendix B, bombers might someday contribute to the antiarmor mission as well, if capable of conducting multiple-aimpoint targeting while loitering over a hostile battlefield. But the above Desert Shield capability does not require those bombers, and indeed an analysis that did require them would have to make optimistic assumptions about future capabilities rather than rely primarily on today's proven systems.

Planning for the Unexpected

But what if efforts at rapid responsiveness, deterrence, arms control, and Desert Shield–like operations somehow failed?[73] What type of U.S. military force structure would be necessary to handle a single conflict rivaling Desert Storm in scope and challenge, should that prove necessary?

Benchmarks from Recent Plans and Experiences

The Pentagon clearly provides its own views on what would be required to establish overwhelming superiority and win decisively in a single Desert Storm–like war. As reflected in the BUR force structure, and stated in the official summary document on the BUR, the administration would plan to employ four to five Army divisions, four to five Marine brigades, about ten Air Force tactical fighter wings as well as one hundred bombers, and four to five aircraft carriers for a single conflict.[74]

Such a force would be smaller than the U.S. contribution to Desert Storm. The U.S. deployment to Desert Storm included a total of about 550,000 military personnel; roughly 8 Army division-equivalents and 2 MEFs, with a total of 2,000 tanks, 2,200 armored personnel carriers, and 1,700 helicopters; 11 land-based tactical fighter wing-equivalents and 6 aircraft carriers, with a total of 1,800 fixed-wing aircraft; 7 submarines; and 2 battleship groups. Other out-of-area militaries, primarily Britain, Egypt, and France, provided roughly 100,000 troops. Additional troops came from Syria, Turkey, and the Gulf Cooperation Council.[75]

But the BUR force for an MRC would probably be at least as effective as the actual Desert Storm force was in 1991, given modernization programs such as Low Altitude Navigation and Targeting Infrared for Night

Table 3-5. Capabilities of U.S. Attack Aircraft Force for One of Two Simultaneous Regional Conflicts under the Alternative Defense Posture

Type of aircraft	Number deployed	Mission	Approximate capabilities[a]	Armored vehicles destroyed per day
Army and Marine attack helicopters	300	Close-air support and ground attack	Up to 16 Hellfire missiles per aircraft, 2 sorties/day	Up to 250
Marine Corps Harriers	50	Close-air support and ground attack	2 to 4 Maverick missiles, 2 sorties/day	50 to 100
Tactical combat aircraft for ground attack (Air Force and possibly some Navy)	300	Ground attack against moving vehicles	Generally 4 to 8 Maverick or laser-guided bombs, 2 sorties/day	500 to 1,000
Tactical combat aircraft for air superiority (Air Force, possibly some Navy)	300	With AWACS and electronic warfare systems, establish air supremacy	None for ground attack, by assumption	0
B-1 and B-52 bombers[b]	140	Attack fixed strategic targets	16 to 24 cruise missiles or 2,000-pound bombs, 1 sortie every 2 days	0
B-2 bombers[b]	16	Attack armor?	30+ tactical munitions dispensers each with about 20 submunitions, 1 sortie every 2 days	Up to 1,000?

Source: Jane's Information Group. *Jane's All the World's Aircraft, 1991-1992* (Alexandria, Va., 1991); Department of Defense. *Conduct of the Persian Gulf War* (April 1992); and Glenn C. Buchan. "The Use of Long-Range Bombers in a Changing World: A Classical Exercise in Systems Analysis," in Paul K. Davis, ed., *New Challenges for Defense Planning: Rethinking How Much Is Enough* (Santa Monica, Calif.: RAND Corporation, 1994), pp. 420–25.

a. The aircraft can carry a wide variety of other weapons, many of which—such as cluster bombs—are useful for attacks against softer armored vehicles. But here the more demanding mission of destroying tanks is generally posited. The availability and performance parameters of next-generation precision-guided munitions are not assumed, except for the case of the B-2 bomber.

b. Bombers are assumed to constitute a "swing force" that could all be devoted to first one conflict and then to another; the numbers here thus assume the availability of the entire bomber force for the conflict at issue.

(LANTIRN) pods, which provide precision attack capabilities for combat aircraft, as well as joint STARS aircraft, which detect and track enemy ground vehicles. The United States now has about 600 aircraft equipped with precision-strike capability, in contrast to a total of less than 200 at the time of the Gulf War, and will have about 1,100 by the year 2000, primarily F-16 aircraft.[76]

In a major conflict, the United States would face an adversary that probably would be weaker than Iraq was in 1990. In particular, Iraq possessed perhaps 5,500 tanks, 7,500 armored personnel carriers or infantry fighting vehicles, 3,500 large-bore artillery weapons, 700 combat aircraft, 160 attack helicopters, and a total of roughly 1,000,000 persons in the armed forces. The BUR reasonably assumes that a future regional opponent would be roughly half to two-thirds as large, particularly in ground forces.[77]

If the leaked Defense Planning Guidance from 1992 is any indication, however, that smaller regional force could be just as capable as the 1990 Iraqi force, which had many units estimated as only one-quarter or one-fifth as good as modern equipment on a tank-for-tank, aircraft-for-aircraft basis. Should future acquisitions involve Western equipment or even top-of-the-line Russian equipment, a smaller foe could have every bit as much capability as Iraq in 1990.[78]

Why A War Could Prove More Difficult than Expected

As argued correctly by the authors of the BUR, it is possible that a regional war could unfold less smoothly than did Desert Storm. In that light, the U.S. reserve force structure is a reassuring insurance policy. What types of conflicts could prove as challenging as Desert Storm, or perhaps even more so? One scenario might entail a catastrophic breakdown of Mideast peace talks together with one or more revolutions in several of the moderate Arab states. As a consequence, most of Israel's frontline neighbors might again ally against it in war. This seems a rather distant prospect, given the divisions within the Arab world as a result of the Gulf War and other developments. But it is still not entirely implausible, in light of the strength of the Islamic fundamentalist movement.

In such a war, the United States would have one very viable military ally but could face adversaries with a combined deployable strength considerably greater than Iraq manifested in 1990. For such an unlikely event, a deployment of three-fourths of the proposed U.S. force structure together with Israel's could achieve force ratios comparable to those the coalition enjoyed against Iraq.

Threats from an adversary's advanced munitions, mines, and weapons of mass destruction could be substantial.[79] Leaving aside the risks of terrorism, which present strategic complications more than warfighting ones, several chief issues remain. One is the vulnerability of large U.S. assets such as ships, ports, airfields, depots, and barracks. Particularly if the United States needed to attempt a forced military entry into a region, aggressors might hope that their possession of mines and the like would lead the American public to pressure its policymakers not to intervene in a conflict for fear of high U.S. casualty rates. The Marines' decision not to stage an amphibious landing in Kuwait, while prudent in light of the fact that it was not necessary, still may give regional aggressors reason to hope that the United States could be deterred from fighting for fear of high casualties. Another question mark concerns the performance of U.S. precision munitions, most of which reportedly could be vulnerable to certain types of sophisticated jamming, and which also depend on potentially vulnerable satellite communications.[80]

Finally, the use of nuclear weapons or other weapons of mass destruction could make for a substantially more difficult and bloody war. The most damaging use of such weapons would probably entail attacks against airfields or ports at times when substantial numbers of U.S. military assets were present. Delivering such weapons would be difficult in a wartime setting, but could not be ruled out. Ballistic missiles or special-forces delivery would probably represent the most likely means. Even without advanced thermonuclear devices, a regional country could probably use fission bombs to delay and complicate a conventional U.S. attack severely.

If an adversary did use weapons of mass destruction, the United States might choose to retaliate in kind, making a second conventional buildup unnecessary. But it would also be wise to retain the ability to defeat the adversary with conventional forces, in case that approach seemed the most sensible—particularly if the enemy had made only a limited strike that caused more material than human loss but complicated war plans significantly.

In the end, predicting demands on U.S. defense forces is an approximate exercise. The BUR's approach is not unreasonable, and it correctly emphasizes a scenario of two regional crises. But it is too pessimistic about the prospects of containing those crises before they erupt into full-fledged war, and too rigid and uncreative about the types of military strategies that might be employed if the crises did deteriorate into conflict. Given that the strategy was devised only after the first Clinton long-term defense budget was proposed, the BUR's intellectual shortcomings are not surprising. But this is all the more reason why the doctrine should be challenged.

Notes

1. William W. Kaufmann, *Assessing the Base Force: How Much Is Too Much?* (Brookings, 1992); Congressional Budget Office, *Limiting Conventional Arms Exports to the Middle East* (September 1992), pp. 82–84; briefing for Brookings by Analytic Sciences Corporation, Rosslyn, Va., February 6, 1995; and John Diamond, "Gen. Luck: NK's Military Deteriorating," *Pacific Stars and Stripes*, January 28, 1995, p. 1.

2. Les Aspin, "Aspin Shows Defense Alternatives," News Release, House Armed Services Committee, February 25, 1992, p. 11.

3. Kaufmann, *Assessing the Base Force*, pp. 54–57; statement of Robert Gates, Director of Central Intelligence, before the Defense Policy Panel of the House Committee on Armed Services, March 27, 1992, pp. 4, 8, 11–16; Les Aspin, Secretary of Defense, *Report on the Bottom-Up Review* (October 1993), p. 13; and International Institute for Strategic Studies, *The Military Balance 1990–1991* (Oxford: Brassey's, 1990), p. 105.

4. See Michael O'Hanlon, "Limiting Conventional Arms Sales to the Persian Gulf," in James Brown, ed., *New Horizons and Challenges in Arms Control and Verification* (Amsterdam: VU University Press, 1994), pp. 99–109.

5. Michael E. O'Hanlon, *The Art of War in the Age of Peace* (Westport, Conn.: Praeger, 1992), p. 69.

6. See, for example, T. N. Dupuy, *Understanding War* (New York: Paragon, 1987), pp. 297–98; T. N. Dupuy, *If War Comes . . . How to Defeat Saddam Hussein* (McLean, Va.: HERO Books, 1991), pp. 53–99; and Joshua M. Epstein, "War with Iraq: What Price Victory?" Brookings Discussion Papers, January 10, 1991.

7. See "China, Former Soviets Can't Match U.S. Fighter Prowess: RAND," *Defense Daily*, April 11, 1995, p. 44.

8. Patrick E. Tyler, "7 Hypothetical Conflicts Foreseen by the Pentagon," *New York Times*, February 17, 1992, p. A1; and Aspin, *Report on the Bottom-Up Review*, p. 14.

9. See Edward N. Luttwak, "Where Are the Great Powers?" *Foreign Affairs*, vol. 73 (July–August 1994), pp. 23–28; and "Conversations with William Perry," *Aerospace America* (October 1994), p. 11.

10. Among the major industrial countries, oil typically accounts for 40 percent to 65 percent of national energy production, but a higher percentage in transportation. See Congressional Budget Office, *Rethinking Emergency Energy Policy* (December 1994), p. 35; World Bank, *World Development Report 1994* (Oxford University Press, 1994), pp. 192–93; and Central Intelligence Agency, *Handbook of International Economic Statistics, 1993* (September 1993), pp. 87–100.

11. "Final Draft of Mobility Requirements Study Update to Go to Services,"

Inside the Pentagon, November 3, 1994, p. 3; Joint Chiefs of Staff, *1991 Joint Military Net Assessment* (Department of Defense, 1991), chap. 9; Aspin, *Report on the Bottom-Up Review*, pp. 19–20; "Conversations with William Perry," p. 11; interview with Secretary of Defense William J. Perry, *Air Force Times*, January 2, 1995, p. 40; and Eric Schmitt, "Some Doubt U.S. Ability to Fight Wars on 2 Fronts," *New York Times*, October 17, 1994, p. 1.

12. Secretary of Defense William J. Perry, *Annual Report to the President and the Congress* (February 1995), p. 219.

13. For a similar argument, see Andrew F. Krepinevich, *The Bottom-Up Review: An Assessment* (Washington: Defense Budget Project, February 1994), pp. 23–24.

14. Aspin, *Report on the Bottom-Up Review*, p. 14.

15. For an argument along these lines, see Krepinevich, *Bottom-Up Review*, pp. 26–27. See also Richard L. Kugler, "Nonstandard Contingencies for Defense Planning," and Kevin N. Lewis, "The Discipline Gap and Other Reasons for Humility and Realism in Defense Planning," in Paul K. Davis, ed., *New Challenges for Defense Planning: Rethinking How Much Is Enough* (Santa Monica, Calif.: RAND Corporation, 1994), pp. 182–85, 131.

16. Aspin, *Report on the Bottom-Up Review*, pp. 13, 19.

17. For a supporting view, see Aspin, "Aspin Shows Defense Alternatives," pp. 23–24.

18. Statement of Robert Gates before Defense Policy Panel of House Committee on Armed Services.

19. President William Clinton, "A National Security Strategy of Engagement and Enlargement" (The White House, July 1994), p. 10.

20. Department of Defense, *Conduct of the Persian Gulf War: Final Report to Congress* (April 1992), pp. E-16–E-24.

21. See Ann Devroy and Thomas W. Lippman, "364 Warplanes Added to Gulf Buildup," *Washington Post*, October 11, 1994, p. 1; and "U.S. Troops Selected for Persian Gulf Duty," *USA Today*, October 11, 1994, p. 2.

22. For further discussion of force-to-space considerations, see Barry R. Posen, "Measuring the European Conventional Balance: Coping with Complexity in Threat Assessment," in Steven E. Miller, ed., *Conventional Forces and American Defense Policy* (Princeton University Press, 1986), p. 106. For a strong criticism of its theoretical underpinnings, see Joshua M. Epstein, *Conventional Force Reductions: A Dynamic Assessment* (Brookings, 1990), pp. 51–64. For a specific discussion of the weather and terrain in eastern Saudi Arabia and Kuwait, see Robert H. Scales, Jr., *Certain Victory: The U.S. Army in the Gulf War* (Washington: Brassey's, 1994), pp. 119–21.

23. See Department of Defense, *Conduct of the Persian Gulf War*, pp. 41–43, 46–51; Scales, *Certain Victory*, pp. 121–28; Thomas A. Keaney and Eliot A. Cohen, *Gulf War Air Power Survey Summary Report* (Government Printing Office, 1993), p. 4; and Michael R. Gordon and Bernard E. Trainor, *The Generals' War: The Inside Story of the Conflict in the Gulf* (Little, Brown, 1995), pp. 123–41.

24. For a mathematical confirmation of this conclusion, see Stephen Biddle, D. Sean Barnett, and David G. Gray, "Stabilizing and Destabilizing Conventional Weapons," IDA Paper P-2548 (Alexandria, Va.: Institute for Defense Analyses, 1991); and Raj Gupta, *Defense Positioning and Geometry* (Brookings, 1993), pp. 25–40. Another real-world application from fairly recent times is the Israeli counteroffensive against Syria in 1973; see U.S. Army, *FM 100–5: Operations* (1993), pp. 6-20–6-22.

25. U.S. Navy, "Carriers for 'Force 2001,'" Spring 1993, p. 6.

26. See CBO, *Limiting Conventional Arms Exports to the Middle East*, pp. 82–84.

27. General Merrill A. McPeak, *Presentation to the Commission on Roles and Missions of the U.S. Armed Forces* (Department of Defense, September 1994), pp. 69, 91–93.

28. Gordon and Trainor, *The Generals' War*, p. 320.

29. General Accounting Office, *Attack Submarines: Alternatives for a More Affordable SSN Force Structure*, NSIAD-95-16 (October 1994); and Robert Holzer, "U.S. Attack Sub Force May Fall to 30 by 2010," *Defense News*, October 3–9, 1994, p. 4.

30. Office of Naval Intelligence, *Worldwide Submarine Proliferation in the Coming Decade* (U.S. Navy, 1995); and International Institute for Strategic Studies, *The Military Balance 1994–1995* (London: Brassey's, 1994).

31. See, for example, Susan Willett, Michael Clarke, and Philip Gummett, "The British Push for the Eurofighter 2000," and Francois Chesnais, Claude Serfati, and Andrew Peach, "The Rafale and French Military-Industrial Autonomy," in Randall Forsberg, ed., *The Arms Production Dilemma* (MIT Press, 1994), pp. 139–59, 193–215.

32. John D. Morrocco, "JAST Contracts Due as Program Recast," *Aviation Week and Space Technology*, November 7, 1994, pp. 27–28.

33. See, for example, John D. Morrocco and David A. Fulghum, "Deficit Thwarts GOP Defense Hike," *Aviation Week and Space Technology*, February 13, 1995, pp. 24–26; Office of the Joint Chiefs of Staff, *1991 Joint Military Net Assessment* (1991), chap. 9; and "European, Central Command Chiefs Identify Challenges for War Strategy," *Inside the Pentagon*, February 16, 1995, p. 2.

34. "After Long Delay, DOD's Mobility Study Ready for Delivery to Congress," *Inside the Pentagon*, March 30, 1995, p. 14.

35. See "Final Draft of Mobility Requirements Study Update to Go to Services," *Inside the Pentagon*, November 3, 1994, p. 3.

36. This estimate is broadly consistent with the historical record: the Soviet Union generally took about three months in preparing its invasions of neighbors, and Iraq took two to three weeks to prepare its 1990 invasion of Kuwait. Similar amounts of warning time were expected for a NATO–Warsaw Pact conflict during the cold war. See, for example, Epstein, *Conventional Force Reductions*, p. 12, based on Office of the Assistant Secretary of Defense for Program Analysis and Evaluation, "NATO Center Region Military Balance Study 1979–1984," Department of Defense, July 13, 1979, p. I-25.

37. Richard K. Betts, *Surprise Attack* (Brookings, 1982), pp. 277–79; Congressional Budget Office, *U.S. Ground Forces: Design and Cost Alternatives for NATO and Non-NATO Contingencies* (1980), p. 69; and Nick Beldecos and Eric Heginbotham, "The Conventional Military Balance in Korea," Massachusetts Institute of Technology, Defense and Arms Control Studies Program, February 1995.

38. Barbara Opall, "U.S. Stockpiles Gear to Meet N. Korean Threat," *Defense News*, March 13–19, 1995, p. 23.

39. Les Aspin, "An Approach to Sizing American Conventional Forces for the Post-Soviet Era," House Committee on Armed Services, February 25, 1992; presentation by Nick Beldecos and Eric Heginbotham, Massachusetts Institute of Technology, at Brookings Institution, March 30, 1995; and Carl Conetta and Charles Knight, "Reasonable Force: Adapting the U.S. Army and Marine Corps to the New Era," pt. 1, Commonwealth Institute, Cambridge, Mass., March 1992, pp. 49–53.

40. Betts, *Surprise Attack*, pp. 3–19.

41. Secretary of Defense Caspar W. Weinberger, *Annual Report to the Congress, Fiscal Year 1987* (February 1986), p. 52.

42. Department of Defense, *Conduct of the Persian Gulf War*, pp. E-20–E-21.

43. *Jane's The World's Fighting Ships, 1990–1991* (Surrey, U.K.: Jane's Information Group, 1990), pp. 787–88.

44. U.S. Transportation Command, *Mobility Requirements Study*, vol. 1 (1992), pp. ES-1–ES-6.

45. Secretary of Defense Les Aspin, *Annual Report to the President and the Congress* (January 1994), p. 20. DOD also plans to keep five Army brigade sets and one Marine brigade set in Europe. It is not clear that the Army pre-positioned sea-based brigade set has found a home; reportedly out of deference to China, Thailand turned down a request to allow U.S. ships to station in its home waters. But even if maritime basing does not prove feasible there, it should be buttressed in Guam, or land-based pre-positioning should be expanded. See Robert Karniol, "Thailand Turns Down U.S. Pre-positioning," *Jane's Defence Weekly*, November 12, 1994, p. 11.

46. See, for example, Department of Defense, *Conduct of the Persian Gulf War*, pp. T-142–T-146.

47. Keaney and Cohen, *Gulf War Air Power Survey Summary Report*, pp. 212–13; and Congressional Budget Office, *Improving Strategic Mobility: The C-17 Program and Alternatives* (September 1986), pp. 44–45.

48. Congressional Budget Office, *Costs of Operation Desert Shield* (January 1991), p. 16.

49. Congressional Budget Office, *Selected Weapons Costs from the President's 1995 Program* (May 1994), p. A-2; and General Jasper Welch, "Analyses of U.S. Requirements for Conventionally Armed Bombers," Northrop-Grumman Corp., July 1994, p. 8.

50. See "Marines Protest Owens' Plan for JROC to Assess Requirement for MPS Ship," *Inside the Pentagon*, November 17, 1994, p. 1; and CBO, *Selected Weapons Costs from the President's 1995 Program*, p. N-6.

51. Tim Shorrock, "Sealift Command to Shift Transport of Jet Fuel to Commercial Ships," *Journal of Commerce*, December 13, 1994, p. 8B.

52. Keaney and Cohen, *Gulf War Air Power Survey Summary Report*, p. 210.

53. Congressional Budget Office, *Rapid Deployment Forces: Policy and Budgetary Implications* (February 1983), pp. 36–38.

54. See Christopher Bowie and others, *The New Calculus: Analyzing Airpower's Changing Role in Joint Theater Campaigns* (Santa Monica, Calif.: RAND Corporation, 1993), pp. 30–32. For analysis of a simultaneous deployment to Korea and Southwest Asia once planned pre-positioning assets and lift assets are added to the U.S. military inventory, see Congressional Budget Office, "Planning for Defense: Affordability and Capability of the Administration's Program," CBO Memorandum (March 1994), p. 26.

55. IISS, *The Military Balance 1994–1995*, p. 30; and Perry, *Annual Report to the President and the Congress*, pp. 218–25.

56. This decision should recognize, the C-17's ability to land on shorter runways than the C-5 and other large aircraft but should not give it great due. According to the General Accounting Office, in regard to the regions of the world where short-warning conflict is of greatest concern to the United States, only six airfields in Korea and one in Saudi Arabia would be usable by C-17s but unusable by C-5s—translating into relative differences of 25 percent and 3 percent, respectively. In each case, the

vast majority of airfields that could be used by one could also be used by the other. See GAO, *Military Airlift: Comparison of C-5 and C-17 Airfield Availability*, NSIAD-94-225 (July 1994), pp. 1–13.

57. Jean R. Gebman, Lois J. Batchelder, and Katherine M. Poehlmann, *Finding the Right Mix of Military and Civil Airlift, Issues and Implications*, vol. 1, Executive Summary (Santa Monica, Calif.: RAND Corporation, 1994), pp. 13–20, 48–55; Bowie and others, *New Calculus*, p. 33; and Perry, *Annual Report to the President and the Congress*, pp. 219–20.

A 747 has an average military payload of about 73 tons and can fly roughly 520 miles an hour for about 10 hours a day. Thus, for a round-trip voyage, it represents about 190,000 ton-miles per day; using 747s to increase the airlift fleet's capacity from 52 million ton-miles per day to 70 million ton-miles per day would therefore require 95 aircraft. A C-17 has about two-thirds the payload, the same speed, and a utilization rate expected to be 50 percent higher, for a nearly identical capacity of 186,000 ton-miles per day; a C-141 has a payload of about 27 tons and roughly the same speed and utilization rate, making for a capacity of about 80,000 ton-miles per day; a C-5 has a payload of about 69 tons and capacity of about 210,000 ton-miles per day; a KC-10 a payload of about 42 tons and capacity of 105,000 ton-miles per day; and a (tactical) C-130 can hold about 12.5 tons and produce 5,000 ton-miles per day of lift. See CBO, *Improving Strategic Mobility*, pp. 44–49.

58. Department of Defense, *Conduct of the Persian Gulf War*, pp. T-88–T-91.

59. Congressional Budget Office, *Reducing the Deficit: Spending and Revenue Options* (March 1994), pp. 56–57.

60. Not all tactical aircraft would need to be refueled in flight in such a crisis; although speed is at a premium in early deployments, even an unrefueled aircraft obliged to land for refueling en route to the Persian Gulf could deploy in about two days, rather than the fifteen hours needed with refueling (provided that bases were available en route). But if it were deemed important to get two to three wings over immediately, the current fleet of KC-10 tankers would be spoken for during the first few days of a deployment. See O'Hanlon, *Art of War in the Age of Peace*, pp. 117–18; and CBO, *Improving Strategic Mobility*, pp. 1–10, 20.

61. Scales, *Certain Victory*, pp. 50–51.

62. Congressional Budget Office, *U.S. Projection Forces: Requirements, Scenarios, and Options* (1978), p. 82.

63. The most difficult type of ferrying operation for tactical combat aircraft would involve trips to the Persian Gulf with a maximum distance between stops of 10,000 kilometers, if no bases in Europe or the Atlantic were available. Over that range, KC-10 aircraft would need about 60 percent of their fuel for themselves, leaving about 60,000 kilograms, or enough fuel for 4 F-15s or roughly 6 F-16s. Thus the augmented KC-10 fleet of 120 aircraft, if devoted to that mission, could fly about 600 aircraft—roughly 8 wing-equivalents—to the destination in one sortie. In other words, the entire deployment could be made in a single sortie requiring about a half day of flight. See O'Hanlon, *Art of War in the Age of Peace*, pp. 116–18.

64. CBO, "Planning for Defense," pp. 27–28, 39–40; and Bowie and others, *New Calculus*, p. 35.

65. Department of Defense, *Conduct of the Persian Gulf War*, p. E-30.

66. See, for example, Keaney and Cohen, *Gulf War Air Power Survey Summary Report*, pp. 210–11.

67. Ibid., p. 57.

68. See, for example, Jeffrey McCausland, *The Gulf Conflict: A Military Analysis* (London: Brassey's, 1993), p. 29.

69. Ibid., p. 31.

70. See Department of Defense, *Conduct of the Persian Gulf War*, pp. T-144–T-145; Christopher F. Foss, ed., *Jane's Armour and Artillery 1991–1992* (Alexandria, Va.: Jane's Information Group, 1991), p. 138; and Scales, *Certain Victory*, pp. 213–320.

71. See Joshua M. Epstein, *Strategy and Force Planning: The Case of the Persian Gulf* (Brookings, 1987), p. 52; and Posen, "Measuring the European Conventional Balance," pp. 114–15.

72. Those sortie rates are less than witnessed in the Gulf War; the rate of usage of precision munitions is greater—in keeping with the ongoing increase in the availability of such munitions and aircraft capable of delivering them—and the estimated effectiveness per precision munition (including laser-guided bombs) of roughly 0.25 is about the same. This latter assumption is quite conservative in light of the expectation that the effectiveness of munitions now in development, such as the brilliant antiarmor submunition and the sensor-fused weapon, will be twice as great as current munitions. Aircraft and helicopters would attack enemy forces with weapons such as Maverick, Hellfire, 30-millimeter cannon, and laser-guided bombs, destroying roughly half of an enemy's forces within a week. In addition, a strategic target set of several hundred aimpoints could be attacked over that same period, partly by tactical combat aircraft and partly by bombers and ships dispensing longer-range cruise missiles.

In the forty days of Operation Desert Storm, coalition air forces flew about 60,000 missions, of which more than 46,000 were attack missions—thus averaging more than 1,000 such missions a day (about 90 percent of them by U.S. aircraft). The bulk of these missions—perhaps two-thirds—were devoted to Iraqi forces in theater, though in the early days of the war the target sets were divided relatively equally among deployed Iraqi forces, strategic targets (with some 3,000 aimpoints in all), and air-control as well as sea-control targets. Some 13,000 precision munitions were used, nearly 10,000 by Air Force aircraft and most of the rest by Army helicopters; more than 100,000 "dumb bombs" were also delivered. The precision munitions were responsible for the majority of the 3,000 to 4,000 vehicles destroyed before the outset of the ground war, implying a destruction probability of nearly 20 percent in that stage of the war (and considerably greater when enemy vehicles were in motion). Department of Defense, *Conduct of the Persian Gulf War*, pp. T-182–T-186, T-18–T-19; Keaney and Cohen, *Gulf War Air Power Survey Summary Report*, pp. 13, 42, 103–15, 197–200; Bowie and others, *New Calculus*, pp. 45, 54–55; Gordon and Trainor, *The Generals' War*, p. 335; Glenn C. Buchan, "The Use of Long-Range Bombers in a Changing World: A Classical Exercise in Systems Analysis," in Davis, ed., *New Challenges for Defense Planning*, pp. 420–21; and John D. Morrocco, "PGM Strategy Faces Budget, Technical Traps," *Aviation Week and Space Technology*, February 27, 1995, p. 45.

73. See, for example, Betts, *Surprise Attack*, pp. 3–24, 87–149.

74. Aspin, *Report on the Bottom-Up Review*, p. 19.

75. Kaufmann, *Assessing the Base Force*, pp. 52–56; Steven R. Bowman, "Persian Gulf War: Summary of U.S. and Non-U.S. Forces," Congressional Research Service, February 11, 1991, pp. 1–8; John M. Collins, "Desert Shield and Desert Storm: Implications for Future U.S. Force Requirements," Congressional Research Service, April 19, 1991, p. 4; and Robert L. Goldrich, "Casualties and Maximum Number of

Troops Employed in Recent U.S. Military Ground Combat Operations," Congressional Research Service, October 8, 1993.

76. McPeak, *Presentation to the Commission on Roles and Missions of the U.S. Armed Forces*, p. 63.

77. International Institute for Strategic Studies, *The Military Balance 1990–1991* (Oxford: Brassey's, 1990), pp. 105–06; and Aspin, *Report on the Bottom-Up Review*, p. 13.

78. See, for example, O'Hanlon, *Art of War in the Age of Peace*, pp. 66–67.

79. For another discussion, see Kugler, "Nonstandard Contingencies for Defense Planning," pp. 165–96; and Krepinevich, *Bottom-Up Review*.

80. See John G. Roos, "A Pair of Achilles' Heels," *Armed Forces Journal International* (November 1994), pp. 21–23; and Morrocco, "PGM Strategy Faces Budget, Technical Traps," pp. 44–47.

CHAPTER FOUR

PEACE OPERATIONS, FORWARD PRESENCE, AND CRISIS RESPONSE

BEYOND THOSE specific countries and security problems that retain an acute importance for the United States, what conceptual framework should guide U.S. policy toward more common and endemic security problems such as civil and ethnic conflict? Those problems have been severe for years and show no signs of abating; if anything, they are worsening. Yet their significance is difficult to evaluate.

In developing a conceptual framework, the administration's 1994 National Security Strategy document provides a useful starting point. It characterizes the likely consequences of rapidly growing populations and deteriorating resource bases in the developing countries as "grave indeed." Those developments have global implications beyond their dire effects on those countries' inhabitants. Particularly in a number of countries in the Middle East, South Asia, and North Africa, direct threats to the West can result from high unemployment, income inequity, politicization of large elements of society, and expanding access to weaponry combined with international terrorist networks. Throughout those regions and in much of the rest of the developing world, growing populations in tandem with weak social and political institutions may threaten the planet's long-term ability to provide food, shelter, heat, and economic opportunity for humanity in general.

In addition, civil warfare in developing countries can sometimes be dangerous for outside parties in a more immediate sense. Rwanda, the former Yugoslavia, and most other conflict-ridden countries such as Sudan, Afghanistan, and Liberia—without nuclear weapons and with only modest likely influence on neighbors—are perhaps not in the category of states that simply must not be allowed to fail. But they are the test cases on which the world is honing its collective approach to problems of civil conflict, and thus they will create lasting legacies that may someday affect the treatment of more serious threats to global security, such as possible civil war in a country possessing nuclear weapons.

Americans cannot reasonably be expected, nor are they willing, to accept a disproportionate share of the global responsibility for peace operations, particularly those that pose little acute threat to international stability. Nor can the world community stumble militarily into virtually all of the world's trouble spots. The enduring nature of global conflict and the longevity of specific conflicts attest to the difficulties of solving deep-rooted antagonisms. A list that includes the Horn of Africa, Sudan, most of Central Africa, Afghanistan, Kurdish territories in Turkey and Iraq, Kashmir, parts of Andean South America, and most of Central America testifies to the vast number that would need to be addressed by a comprehensive strategy.[1]

U.S. forces are not even immune to what happens in blue beret operations that do not directly involve them. U.S. capabilities often are used to deploy other countries' troops, provide them with information on the unfolding of military developments, or provide backup of some sort in case a mission goes awry.

It is worth bearing in mind the useful cautionary words of former Secretary of Defense Caspar Weinberger, whose principles on the use of U.S. military force favored either noninvolvement or all-out combat with clearly defined and commonly accepted links to major U.S. interests.[2] General Colin Powell and others in the military have tended to support this position. Lethal force should never be used casually. But several recent military operations, including those in Haiti, northern Iraq, Panama, and Libya, have had more limited yet important aims. The remarkable successes of recent multilateral diplomacy and peace operations in places such as Cambodia, El Salvador, and Southern Africa also suggest that the proper combination of circumstances, timing, and external forces can break the cycle of conflict. Doing so is important; the developing world is, in the long run, too important to global stability to be ignored.

In fact, in the end, most people do not accept the Weinberger and Powell maxims as absolute or universal. Even recent Republican calls for the use of air strikes in Bosnia and Herzegovina suggest a level of U.S. military involvement that falls somewhere between peace and war, despite the protestations from some of the same prominent Republicans against becoming involved in conflicts that do not involve major U.S. interests.[3] Moreover, when in power in the White House, Republicans

Table 4-1. Casualties in Recent U.S. Military Combat

Action and date	Casualties				Maximum U.S. troop strength
	Killed in action or died of wounds	Wounded in action	Prisoner of war or missing in action	Total	
Somalia (1992–October 6, 1993)	23	143	1 prisoner of war	167	25,800
Persian Gulf War (1991)	148	467	23	638	541,000
Panama (1989–90)	23	324	0	347	22,500
Lebanon (1982–84)	266	169	1	436	1,900
Grenada (1983)	19	115	0	134	8,800

Source: Robert L. Goldich. "Casualties and Maximum Number of Troops Deployed in Recent U.S. Military Ground Combat Actions." Congressional Research Service, October 8, 1993.

also have tended to use various military instruments to try to shape events in other countries. Under President Bush shows of force and military-assisted relief operations multiplied steadily over time.[4] Thus political realities and the new shape of the international security environment argue against a strict application of the all-or-nothing school of U.S. military deployments.[5] The military services, to their credit, generally accept the need to prepare for a wide range of engagements. They also are aware of the likelihood of casualties even in limited uses of force (see table 4-1 for an account of casualties in recent U.S. military operations).[6]

This view is not an argument for doing the impossible or the herculean. Rather, it suggests that the United States, generally in tandem with other countries, should selectively yet ambitiously try to address most forms of serious organized armed conflict around the world.[7] In some cases, doing so might entail helping parties negotiate and establish a peace. In others, it could involve simply mitigating the effects of war through the creation of safe havens or humanitarian relief zones; in occasional cases, it could involve helping a new government fend off armed resistance from an extremist movement that refused to become party to a peace accord.[8] That doing so is legitimate under international law, consistent with human rights principles as well as principles of national self-determination, and morally justifiable is also increasingly argued by scholars across a wide political and academic spectrum.[9]

What does all of this mean for military planning? The issues are of several types: peacetime presence operations, military force structure, and collaboration with other countries' forces.

U.S. Peacetime Presence

For decades, the U.S. Navy and Marine Corps have maintained routine naval deployment patterns in peacetime. Variations have occurred in typical deployment levels, but major theaters—in particular, the Western Pacific, Mediterranean, Indian Ocean, and Persian Gulf areas—have generally been the object of continuous attention of one form or another.[10]

Land-based forward presence also has been a fixture of post–World War II U.S. military policy. But U.S. forces, which numbered 300,000 in Europe during the cold war, will be scaled back to 100,000 by the end of fiscal year 1995. In the absence of a resolution of the Korean standoff, forces in East Asia have been reduced less and remain around 100,000— primarily Army and Air Force personnel in South Korea as well as Marines, Navy, and Air Force personnel in Japan.[11]

In this context, should sea deployments remain essentially as they have been, particularly at a time when peace operations and related missions are placing new demands on the Navy and Marine Corps? This question is being asked increasingly within the Pentagon, if not yet among most security analysts on Capitol Hill and elsewhere.[12]

The deterrent benefits of the routine peacetime presence mission were called into question even during the cold war.[13] It was not clear why continuous aircraft carrier presence was needed when ships could be "surged" into theaters of crisis fairly quickly—especially since serious crises required reinforcement by a second or third carrier group from American ports.[14] Moreover, presence is never truly continuous vis-à-vis a given country; a carrier near the Philippines, for example, is several days' sail from countries like Thailand or Bangladesh and over a week away from the Persian Gulf. Conventional wisdom about three-to-one rules notwithstanding, it generally takes about five ships in the fleet for every one on deployment because of the need to transit from the United States to a theater of deployment, allow for periodic ship overhauls, and avoid keeping sailors at sea more than 50 percent of the time (see figure 4-1).[15] In light of this undesirable efficiency ratio, the forward-presence mission has been a particularly expensive one for the U.S. military.

Some tense situations do argue for a continuous show of resolve on the part of U.S. sea-based forces—particularly in cases where allies or friends are skittish about being associated too closely with Washington,

Figure 4-1. Carrier Force Levels and Overseas Presence
Number of carriers

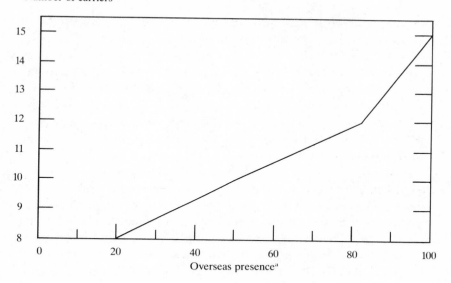

Overseas presence[a]

Source: Les Aspin, *Report on the Bottom-Up Review* (October 1993), p. 50.
a. The percentage presence in two regions, assuming a full-time presence in a third region.

significant threats to important U.S. interests are acute, and potential adversaries might reasonably doubt the degree of Washington's readiness to fight for its interests. Such a situation describes well the security situation in the Persian Gulf area during the late 1970s and 1980s, for example.[16] Having at least some vessels on forward deployment at all times also is important for providing routine security for maritime pre-positioned ships and escorting them in any crisis that they might be called upon to handle. Finally, it provides the means to conduct exercises with a number of allies. Given the primarily symbolic purpose of routine deployments, however, there are good reasons to consider using Marine ships or naval vessels such as destroyers to provide routine presence in those settings, saving carriers for crises, occasional peacetime deployments in support of military exercises, or other special and specific requirements.[17]

Crisis deployments have often involved two or three carriers: for example, during wars between India and Pakistan or Israel and its neighbors, during turning points of the Vietnam War, or in various crises between the Koreas or the Chinas. Three carriers assembled in a task force for a major regional crisis, although not enough combat power to undertake major sustained wartime operations, probably provide a combined air capability at least the equal of that of any regional power except China and also have the capability to undertake specific combat operations such as air patrol or a limited ground attack. The Suez and Cuban missile crises involved eight carriers each; the Gulf War, six.[18] According to standard deterrence theory, the goal of the United States in many of these situations was to show leaders in Moscow or Beijing—countries that it could not afford to fight but also could not afford to appease— that it was willing to engage in a crisis-reaction process and risk escalation in order to protect certain interests.[19]

Today, crisis response is much more likely to be directed at a strictly regional audience and to have as its real purpose the deployment of locally significant amounts of combat power. Given the multitude of land-based tools available for use in theaters such as the Persian Gulf and Korea, the need to employ naval forces can be questioned. In such cases, the Air Force correctly argues that ten land-based tactical fighter wings could be deployed more rapidly than—and at least as economically as— four fighter wings on a total of four aircraft carrier battle groups (see figure 4-2).[20]

Recent U.S. naval and Marine deployments in the Adriatic, Caribbean, Persian Gulf, and Indian Ocean have been sized and shaped for the concrete purposes of enforcing blockades, preparing for invasions, adding a locally significant amount of airpower to a regional balance, or being on call should UN forces run into trouble when withdrawing.[21]

In today's world, moreover, local crises in the developing world involve internal conflict much more commonly than international tensions. In that context, stand-off attack from ships or planes will not generally be effective; the most important tool for responding to crises is, and is likely to remain, real capability on the ground. Ground forces can protect populations, distinguish combatants from noncombatants, police cease-fires, and attempt to separate combatants. In the present global information age, worldwide legal and political principles are upheld less by the continuous presence of a carrier or Marine unit that the United States or some other country may or may not be prepared to actually use and more by the track record of the international community in responding resolutely to internal conflicts wherever they might arise.

This situation could change: for example, the Saudi and perhaps even the Kuwaiti regimes could come under increasing domestic pressure to

Figure 4-2. Annual Operating Cost of Land-Based and Sea-Based Tactical Aircraft
Millions of dollars

Source: General Merrill A. McPeak, *Presentation to the Commission on Roles and Missions of the Armed Forces* (Department of Defense, September 1994), p. 190.

a. The shaded area indicates the cost of operating the aircraft carrier; the white area indicates the cost of operating the aircraft on it.

distance themselves again from the West, with an associated loss of land access for the United States. Yet the West would still have a strong interest in demonstrating continued commitment to those countries' security in order to deter any Iraqi or Iranian aggression. At such a stage, the Navy might become more important for occasional presence and crisis response than it appears to be today. This suggests retaining some capability to return to prolonged periods of deployments.

An Alternative Aircraft Carrier Force Structure

On balance, it is worthwhile to keep a number of carriers; they do provide secure and reliable airfields with moderately rapid responsiveness. But they seem unlikely to be needed as much in the future as in the past, and their operational patterns can be changed substantially.

A fleet of eight carriers would preserve a strong naval capability for crisis response. This fleet would also be adequate for regional war, as argued in chapter 3.[22] Normally, on average one or two carriers would be on mission, either conducting exercises, aiding in a blockade, providing a show of strength, or otherwise supporting U.S. security goals. If necessary, the fleet could maintain a continuous carrier presence in a single region such as the Persian Gulf during a tense period.

Marine Corps Operations

Similar arguments apply to Marine Corps presence. Specific missions such as backing up UN forces or resolutions could often substitute for routine presence. But if such missions were not occurring, deployments of the modest Marine expeditionary units could still be undertaken, roughly one at a time in either the Mediterranean or Indian Ocean regions. Thus the capability to respond to crises that might require extraction of embassy personnel or similar activities would be available within several days' sailing time of most potential hot spots; in addition, some exercises could be conducted with other countries' forces. Marine Corps General John Sheehan, commander in chief of U.S. forces in the Atlantic Ocean region, recently suggested an operational pattern with a similar flexibility.[23]

Were rapid delivery of ordnance required somewhere, strategic bombers or possibly tactical combat aircraft could be used. Were a more rapid U.S. presence on the ground deemed necessary, special forces or airborne forces could be deployed by aircraft from the United States.

Other Shipborne Assets and Operations

There are other ways the Navy could relieve stress on its other vessels and crews. For example, as argued in a recent report by the Center for Naval Analyses, it would be sensible to consider applying a crew-rotation policy to ships that are deployed overseas. A given ship would stay on forward station for roughly two years, then return home for repairs and rotation. Crews would be flown overseas to join their ships, relieving crews already there, who would then be flown home.

In order to be true to Navy policy of limiting the duration of any individual's overseas deployment to six months at a stretch and overall deployment time to no more than 50 percent over a twenty-month period, four separate "shifts" would man the ships during that two-year deployment period. For any given ship based overseas, an average of 2.5 ships would still be needed. In addition to the vessel on deployment, one would provide training facilities (and warfighting backup capability) in home waters, and on average "one-half" ship would be in repair. This type of scheme would reduce by 50 percent the number of vessels needed to maintain a given level of forward deployment.[24]

How many ships might the United States need to deploy at once around the world for specific missions? Recently, vessels have been used for blockades or similar activities in support of United Nations resolutions in different parts of the world. For much of 1994, for example, operations were under way in the Adriatic, Red Sea, Persian Gulf, and Caribbean, entailing some twenty-five to thirty surface combatants.[25] In the early 1990s, the United States had an average of about thirty major surface combatants deployed at a time, split in roughly equal proportions among the Western Pacific, Indian Ocean–Persian Gulf area, and Mediterranean; in the 1980s, average deployment levels frequently reached forty ships.[26] These data suggest that future global deployments under the suggested concept of operations would generally average no more than thirty ships; even if they did surge above that level at some point, an average of greater than forty ships would be unlikely. It should thus adequate for the Navy to have a fleet of roughly 100 major surface combatants rather than the 115 or so envisioned under the BUR.

Submarines

What about the submarine fleet? The BUR suggests that it should be in the range of forty-five to fifty-five vessels, primarily of a class more advanced than the Los Angeles but less expensive than the new Seawolf class. It also states that peacetime presence operations are more demanding than wartime requirements, as with the carrier fleet. Presence operations are viewed as taxing for a fleet of forty-five SSNs (attack submarines) and would be excessive for a fleet much smaller. The BUR also states that a fleet of thirty SSNs would be insufficient for either presence or warfighting requirements.[27] Such conclusions seem consistent with the pattern of cold war submarine deployment, in which perhaps fourteen attack submarines were deployed at a time on their own—half to trail Soviet ballistic missile submarines and half to conduct other reconnaissance and espionage activities—and some six to eight submarines were deployed to accompany carrier battle groups. With a duty cycle of about 33 percent, around sixty submarines would be needed for those purposes.[28]

But the mission of trailing Russian SSBNs (ballistic missile submarines) now seems inconsistent with the basic U.S. imperative of helping

Russia retain a viable nuclear deterrent economically and securely, and thus it should be ended. Moreover, there should no longer be any residual concern about protecting the choke points leading out of the Sea of Okhotsk and Sea of Japan as well as those found along the Greenland-Iceland-United Kingdom gap. During the cold war, the size of Soviet conventional armies made it imperative that the United States not lose forces and supplies on the way to Europe to support a NATO conventional defense. Today, the combined strength of European NATO countries alone probably exceeds that of Russia, once one accounts for the maintenance levels of equipment and training of troops.[29]

Such a reduction in U.S. attack submarine missions would make it possible to conduct routine presence and reconnaissance with a fleet of some twenty vessels and to escort aircraft carriers with a total of about eight SSNs. This analysis leads to a U.S. attack submarine fleet of about thirty to thirty-five ships, of which a "silver-torpedo" force of some ten Seawolf or new attack submarines would be teamed with improved Los Angeles–class submarines (either overhauled or produced afresh in the future). Such a fleet would be far more capable than that of any regional power, including China (which has about fifty operational submarines, but only five nuclear-powered and most of the rest obsolescent) and North Korea (twenty-five submarines, all diesel and obsolescent). Given the ready availability of bombers and surface ships to assist in any large-scale cruise missile attack such as that of the Gulf War, in which some 250 conventionally armed cruise missiles were fired, submarines would not need to assume primary responsibility for such a mission. Even a small fleet could provide ample capability for the one thing submarines can do most effectively: contribute to a completely unexpected and localized surprise attack. Thus such a fleet would seem to meet all necessary requirements for post–cold war U.S. security policy (see table 4-2 for a list of these and other possible changes in the U.S. military force structure relevant to forward presence and peace operations).

Peace Operations and the U.S. Military

Are new types of military units or different mixes of units needed for peace operations? Apart from several specific and modest changes in training, many of which are already being put in place, major changes do not appear necessary in the basic types of building blocks in the U.S.

Table 4-2. An Alternative Defense Posture for Forward Presence and Peace Operations

Type of program or unit	BUR	Alternative
Suggested cuts		
Major surface combatants	110–116	100
Active army light divisions	5	4
Marine Corps fighter wing-equivalents	5	2
Air Force tactical combat wings	20	18
Aircraft carrier battle groups and air wings	12/11	8/7
Marine Corps V-22 aircraft	425	0
Attack submarines	45–55	35
Suggested increases		
Marine Corps pre-positioned brigade sets[a]	3	4
Army pre-positioned brigade sets[a]	4	6
Marine CH-46/CH-53 helicopters or equivalent	0	375
UN training and equipment programs	No	Yes

a. In or near Korea and Southwest Asia.

military. But some fine-tuning may be useful. In addition, despite the BUR's suggestions to the contrary, a single unit should probably not have primary responsibility for both regional warfighting and peace operations.

Air Units

In many ways, peace operations and other UN Security Council–motivated operations of the U.S. military in 1994 have centered on air missions of one form or another, be they airdrops in Bosnia, airlifts into Zaire in response to the Rwanda tragedy, or enforcement of no-fly zones in Bosnia and Iraq. In addition, the Air Force would have had an important role in any airborne assault in Haiti, and its deployment of tactical combat aircraft to Kuwait and environs was a key element in the U.S. response to threatening Iraqi troop movements in October 1994.

Such operations were rather taxing to certain F-15, AWACS, and airlift crews, but were not taxing for the service as a whole and were not deemed unsustainable by the Air Force. The Air Force chief of staff stated last fall that, despite the fact that some troops had been deployed for 150 days or more in the last year (more than the preferred limit of 120 days), today's troop morale levels are good and reenlistment rates high.[30] Still, there were problems associated with such deployments, evidenced in higher levels of family and alcohol abuse, as conveyed to Secretary Perry by Brigadier General John Dallager in Germany in October. Using forces

normally based in the United States for some missions would help mitigate such stresses. In some specific cases, such as for AWACS, added
crews might prove helpful, too.[31]

In addition, many peace operations probably could be performed by
less capable aircraft than F-15s. In conflicts in Africa or the poorer
countries of Central Asia, any needed air cover would be rare and min-
imal, and almost certainly could be handled by aircraft such as F-16s and
A-10s or the air forces of other modern militaries.

What of airlift operations? Because the United States already has a
large airlift fleet, and because under the strategy recommended here it
would enhance it further, even demanding humanitarian and peace operations would not drive the size of the fleet. A fleet that was considered
"broken" from the point of view of regional war nevertheless delivered
record-setting amounts of supplies to Bosnia and Rwanda in recent years.
Still, to help that fleet recover, and to provide for a more concrete expression of burden sharing and cooperative security, other countries and in
particular those of NATO Europe should be better equipped with airlift
assets (not only for peace operations but in order to help more effectively
with regional warfighting if necessary, as discussed further in chapter 6).

Ground Forces

Consider first the matter of timing. Training forces for peace operations, while somewhat specialized, does not require so much of a unit's
time or attention that it is fundamentally incompatible with honing warfighting skills.[32] Where they are straightforward, peacekeeping and monitoring do not require particularly highly trained soldiers (though these
soldiers do need some regional political expertise and sensitivity), as
evidenced in successful operations over the years in places such as the
Sinai.

Where they are challenging, peacekeeping missions are generally difficult because they involve special skills such as policing and civil affairs
or because they could involve combat. For the former requirements, the
discussion below about special-purpose units applies; some modest increases in certain types of active-duty military units do seem appropriate.
In the latter case, traditional military skills—or at least certain types,
such as urban warfare, other types of infantry combat, and maintaining
local security—are critical.[33] Although not typically high intensity, such
combat is challenging and part of normal training requirements for U.S.

troops. This is particularly true for the Marine Corps, special forces, and some light Army forces, whose core missions are to provide flexibility across a wide range of possible levels of conflict. As stated in a Marine Corps manual:

> The Marine Corps, as the nation's force in readiness, must have the versatility and flexibility to deal with military and paramilitary situations across the entire spectrum of conflict. This is a greater challenge than it may appear; conflicts of low intensity are not simply lesser forms of high-intensity war. A modern military force capable of waging a war of high intensity may find itself ill-prepared for a "small" war against a poorly equipped guerrilla force.[34]

Supporting this argument further is the fact that there is now, much more than in earlier eras of U.S. military training and doctrine, a body of experienced peacekeepers that is kept sharp through experience and training.[35] The exemplary performance of U.S. military personnel in Haiti and Somalia would seem to vindicate this judgment. Even in Somalia, the mission's limited success was arguably not in any way caused by a lack of proper skills among the rank and file of the military, but rather by a dubious judgment on the part of top-level political and military leadership in the United States and United Nations that warlord Aidid could be quickly isolated and arrested.[36]

Do peace operations require more of some types of existing units than others? Peace operations tend to place greater relative requirements upon light infantry forces and certain types of special operations forces, such as police units, than do preparations for regional war. Were one to develop from scratch strategies and force postures that made fundamental distinctions between preparing for peace operations and preparing for major combat, quite different types of U.S. military forces might result. In particular, taken to their logical extremes, the former force posture would have a substantially higher fraction of light units than would the latter. This can be seen in the BUR's notional 50,000-strong force for peace operations, which includes one air assault or airborne division, one light infantry division, one Marine expeditionary brigade, one to two carrier battle groups, one to two composite wings of Air Force aircraft, special operations forces, civil affairs units, airlift and sealift forces, and combat support and service support units.[37]

As a practical matter, however, regional warfighting requirements will not disappear, and thus a certain number of heavy divisions will remain necessary. Moreover, the BUR, with its priority on preparing for regional conflict, still retains several divisions' worth of light forces—Army and

Marine Corps combined—for warfighting purposes. They provide key mobility, flexibility, and suitability for activities such as urban warfare, military occupation, mountain or cold-weather warfare, and protection of flanks.[38] The analysis of chapter 3 argues that at least two division-equivalents of Marines and two of Army light forces seem useful to retain for regional conflict scenarios. The record of the Gulf War highlights the effectiveness of air assault forces in maneuvers, as well as the usefulness of at least a certain amount of airborne capability for setting up a tripwire force early in a crisis. (This is perhaps less the case in Korea or Southwest Asia, given the permanent pre-positioning of U.S. forces there now, than for some unexpected crisis elsewhere.)

The question, then, would seem to be, do possible peacekeeping missions require some or all of the following Army and Marine units: a third active Marine division, a division-size 82d Airborne, the 10th Mountain Division, and the 25th Infantry Division? In a nutshell, my answer is that it is important to keep the bulk of these units, but it should be possible to reduce the size of the Army light divisions to roughly two active brigades each, for a net reduction of one Army light division-equivalent. Doing so would retain the special capabilities and geographic coverage offered by the three divisions together, but reduce their size in recognition of the fact that demands upon them are unlikely to require all their current assets.

To assess needs for light forces, one must attempt to foresee the likely—and desirable—frequency and scope of U.S. military participation in future peace operations. At present, it seems doubtful that the scope of any direct U.S. role in them will become much greater in the future. Political momentum seems to be in precisely the opposite direction; policymakers in the United States and some other countries are wary of large, open-ended multilateral peace operations.[39] Moreover, the world community is already engaged in trying to control about half of the world's thirty to thirty-five conflicts (a number that has remained roughly constant for many years).[40] And in trying to develop a fair and politically sustainable concept of an international division of labor, one tends to arrive at the conclusion that the United States should not take the military lead in most expanded approaches to peace operations when it already plays the role of effective guarantor of some of the more important and difficult missions.[41]

What then might be the U.S. military requirements for a more ambitious global approach to conflict resolution and peace operations? As one way of addressing the question of how much peace operations could increase, assume that the number of conflicts around the world will remain roughly thirty-five in number for the foreseeable future, consistent with historical trends, at least until a substantial number of attempts at peace operations succeed.[42] If vigorous attempts were made to push most toward solution, the current number that seem amenable to peace monitoring, peacekeeping, or peace enforcement might increase to two-thirds or three-fourths of the total.

If the new missions together had on average the same character as existing ones, the total number of UN forces might reach 100,000 or, depending on the nature of the missions, possibly approach 150,000 at times. Direct U.S. participation in those missions might generally remain modest and tied to cases where the United States had a special interest or where its presence carried a desirable political weight. But, by analogy with current operations, the total number of U.S. forces in indirect support of such missions might number as many as 40,000 ground units and a total of 40,000 air and sea units. (Excluding the troops in Korea, which support a unique UN resolution and mission rather than a blue-helmeted mission, some 30,000 to 40,000 U.S. troops support peace operations at present.)[43]

Given this requirement, what should Marine Corps forces look like? With three divisions in the Corps, as is the case now, even if 30,000 to 40,000 Marines were deployed in support of peace operations, roughly two division-equivalents of Marine forces would remain on call for flying to a regional crisis to "marry up" with their pre-positioned equipment. Thus, under this approach, U.S. decisionmakers would not have to choose between abandoning a sensitive and delicate peace operation on the one hand and slowing the U.S. response to two simultaneous major crises on the other. Such an approach provides a 3:1 rotation base for the Marines: two division-equivalents generally at home, available if necessary for responding to major regional crises, and one division-equivalent on deployment in support of a UN mission, bilateral exercises, or, if circumstances permit, a routine deployment.

Today, the 10th, 82d, and 25th Army divisions could provide more than 50,000 personnel, including those in support roles. The total of all of those individuals would be ample to provide a rotation base for a U.S. Army deployment in peace operations of up to 20,000 individuals. Dropping a brigade from each division, as suggested here, would leave the Army able to sustain some 15,000 troops in peace operations indefinitely and without undue strain. When combined with Marine forces, the total sustainable U.S. ground capability for peace operations would exceed 50,000 individuals, considerably more than the likely demand. Even if major regional combat broke out at the same time, at least one of the light divisions, if not both, could be left in place in their peace operations, since all heavy forces, two Marine divisions, and at least three light division-equivalents would remain available. (My alternative U.S. active force posture would include at least eleven divisions, of which six might be required for a Desert Storm–like war, three for a Desert Shield–like operation, and thus two still available for other purposes.)

A single large peace operation in which U.S. troops took part could, however, drive up demands further. (For example, the Bosnia mission as envisioned in late 1994 might have required 25,000 U.S. troops or even more.)[44] However, such an operation would probably involve at least some heavy forces. Since the recommended force posture would retain two heavy divisions that would not be deployed initially under the "simultaneous Desert Shield strategy," they could be placed into a peace operation without fear of harming initial U.S. military responsiveness for more traditional conflicts. Thus, all things considered, U.S. ground forces with eight active Army divisions and three active Marine Corps divisions should be able to handle a quite substantial number of UN peace operations.

Modest Changes in U.S. Force Structure

Despite the overall conclusion that a military force structure suited for regional war will have the basic types of ingredients needed for peace operations, some changes in U.S. force structure would be helpful.

It seems sensible to put a number of civil affairs units in the active forces, where they are more easily accessible for extended periods. Specific types of units that should probably be transformed at least in part into active-duty forces include water supply battalions (all 5 are in guard or reserve units today), judge advocate general units (all 141 are guard or reserve), public affairs units (all 74 are guard or reserve), and civil affairs units (36 of 37 are in the guard or reserves).[45]

What number of those units, and how many people, might sensibly be made active duty? A rough guide can be obtained by reference to recent large peace and humanitarian operations of the United Nations. Several thousand military police and observers were deployed in Cambodia at the height of the UN mission there, for example. As of mid-1994, some 1,300 military police were deployed worldwide by the United Nations, most in Bosnia. (Those units were not, however, American.) Some 3,000 U.S. logistics personnel were in Somalia at a representative point in the mission in 1993, and a somewhat smaller number of U.S. special-purpose personnel were deployed to Rwanda in 1994.[46] A more detailed analysis than can be offered here would be required to determine exactly how much different types of units should be bolstered, but all told the likely requirement for such U.S. units seems unlikely to exceed 5,000 or so, even if the United States plays a greater role in providing such units than it has in the past.

Peace Operations and Multilateral Force Planning Issues

In addition to questions about the U.S. military's proper role in peace operations, there are other matters with important bearing on the future of multilateral security operations. How should the international community work to broaden the role of other countries—particularly poorer developing countries—in peace operations? Would any changes in the ways UN peace operations are funded improve the workings of those operations at a reasonable cost?

Training Centers and Standardized Equipment

Of the 70,000 peacekeepers in the world in late 1994, slightly more than one-third were from the Western industrialized countries, some 6,000 from the former Warsaw Pact bloc, and the rest from developing countries—largely countries of the Indian subcontinent, but including a wide representation. These troops vary greatly in their military competence, training, and equipment.[47] Missions requiring a substantial contingent of modern military forces are thus generally infeasible unless the Western powers are willing to provide substantial ground and, when necessary, air units.

UN EQUIPMENT STOCKS AND TRAINING. To some degree, the UN's dependence on the world's better militaries will endure as long as a wide divergence remains in the overall competence of different defense establishments. But improving the peacekeeping abilities of a number of developing countries could yield a substantial return for a modest amount of effort and expenditure. An ambitious yet not unreasonable effort might establish one or two regional peacekeeping training centers, perhaps in Africa and South Asia, and also expand the UN's equipment stocks in Pisa, Italy. Together, these actions would attempt to increase the pool of responsive and competent forces available to the United Nations. Such an expanded pool of peacekeepers could help in situations such as those occurring in 1994 in Rwanda and the Zairian refugee camps, in which countries were often willing or able—but generally not both at once—to take steps to halt genocide.[48]

Were some of the trained soldiers from nearby countries, their governments might—because of geographical proximity and solidarity, economic interest, concern over refugee flows, or other reasons—be more inclined than distant powers to become involved in a given peace operation. (In some cases, however, one would have to be careful about using peacekeepers from immediately neighboring countries, depending on the historical backdrop, ethnic overlaps between countries, and other factors.) In some such conflicts, the links between great-power security interests and what transpires within a given country or region, though real, may not always be strong. Since some two-thirds of the world's armed conflicts tend to be outside the regions of greatest concern to the Western world, a regional division of labor at peacekeeping and peace enforcement would seem to be a necessary prerequisite to effective resolution of global conflicts.[49]

This idea would be similar to that advanced by Britain, France, and several French-speaking African countries in 1994. Those countries proposed to provide training and logistics support to some military units from African countries in order to form regional capabilities for peace operations.[50] This idea is also similar to a recent suggestion of the secretary general of the United Nations.[51] Sending troops, and perhaps also mechanics and other technicians, to training centers could be made a necessary precondition for eligibility for participation in peacekeeping missions. Those missions are a financially attractive activity for many militaries to which it would not be unreasonable to attach at least some strings.[52]

Important challenges would face any effort to carry out such a systematic use of training centers and equipment stocks. It would be incumbent on the United Nations and its members to make sure that equipment was purchased in ways that allowed for an efficient, coordinated, top-quality force, and that training centers not simply be located in countries that were able to curry favor in United Nations corridors. Problems of patronage and inefficiency continue to exist in the UN procurement and personnel system today; if not directly addressed, they would probably doom any major new initiative politically and technically.[53] One important way of countering countries' parochial concerns might be to use a multinational commission of esteemed former officials of national governments and the United Nations, loosely patterned after the base closure commission in the United States, to make overall recommendations for equipment inventories and training centers to achieve the goals of efficiency, economy, diversity, and yet compatibility. Another challenge would be lining up the requisite transport capabilities, an area in which it is unfair and undesirable to depend entirely on the United States.

Even under such an approach, the United States and some other powers might implicitly bear responsibility for backing up, or at least extracting, a force that proved incapable of completing its mission or assuring its own survival. Thus improving units from other countries would not change the basic fact that the United States or another major military power probably would still need to be willing to confer a certain approval on difficult peace operations. Under worst-case assumptions, their direct military support might also be needed even if not initially planned.[54]

Nevertheless, such forces would provide a key advantage: especially for those conflicts that seem likely to remain geographically contained and far removed from the major powers, the international community would develop an alternative between doing nothing and doing more than Western governments ultimately could ask their citizens to support.[55] In many cases, the most compelling recent example being the genocide in Rwanda, the weapons of indigent forces are modest in quantity and quality, yet the scale of destruction they can wreak is immense and the humanitarian crises they can engender are massive.[56] In such settings, forging a durable political resolution of conflict may be implausible at first, but the international community may wish to do what it can to protect civilians and otherwise limit the damage that intense civil war can do to humans, societal institutions, and a country's future prospects.

A SPECIFIC APPROACH. One idea for improving UN response capabilities for civil wars might be to establish the equivalent of some five brigades' worth of moderately heavy combat capability and another ten brigades of lighter infantry equipment. Under this scheme, the United Nations would store the equipment at central depots and training centers, joining it up with national forces only for training or actual UN missions. Battalions or brigades of troops from participating countries' military establishments would rotate to each of two or three centers for training sessions lasting roughly one month. This scheme would produce a callable list of some thirty brigade-equivalents of troops from perhaps twenty to fifty countries in all. It would result in the availability of around 100,000 trained troops for missions that at present involve roughly 30,000 troops and ten brigades from developing countries. Brigades that did not need UN equipment might still visit the centers for training rotations.

The value of the equipment might reach about $5 billion, but initially much of it might be acquired less expensively because of the surplus of older military equipment in the inventories of several major military powers today. Over time, though, $5 billion would need to be spent by the international community roughly every twenty-five years to sustain such an equipment stock.[57]

Operating and maintaining the equipment and training forces from a wide variety of countries might entail as much as $1 billion a year in additional expense (using per capita Marine Corps figures for operations and maintenance as a rough guide).[58] Adding in equipment costs, the overall international financial burden could thus average slightly more than $1 billion annually, of which the U.S. share might total $300 million. (Alternatively, Japan and Germany—countries unlikely to provide substantial troop contributions to peace operations in the near future, yet quite financially able—could supply the bulk of those funds.)[59] With such an effort, the world community would create a number of well-trained units that could quickly deploy to crises to restore civil order, or, depending on circumstances, at least establish safe havens for beleaguered populations.

The Allied Role

A number of European countries—notably Britain, France, and the Scandinavian countries—as well as Canada have been important contributors to peacekeeping historically. Several of these countries have helped push along the state of knowledge and practice on matters such as peacekeeping training.[60]

A positive new development to help such militaries coordinate operations in this context is NATO's Combined Joint Task Force. It is a flexible approach for commanding, controlling, and supplying various permutations of forces from NATO and Partnership-for-Peace nations in a variety of potential peace operations. If taken seriously and actually employed, it would also help provide a persuasive raison d'être to an alliance that otherwise runs the risk of obsolescence. The French-German–based Eurocorps also provides a 40,000-strong force structure that could be used for rapid-response deployments in support of UN operations, particularly in light of the German Constitutional Court's decision in 1994 to permit deployments of its country's troops outside of NATO even if for reasons other than the immediate defense of allied territory.[61]

Two additional steps would also be helpful at this stage. First, other NATO countries, acting collectively under the auspices of NATO or the West European Union (WEU) or individually, could emphasize logistics and support forces more heavily in their procurement policies and force planning. Japan should consider doing so as well, so that those countries together could take some burden off the United States. Transport aircraft may be the most important need; a number of others, such as water purification and shipping systems, are also worthy of attention. In this light, the United States should welcome rather than resist attitudes such as that expressed by France's permanent representative to the WEU:

> Access to the Alliance's collective assets does not necessarily exempt the Europeans from making their own defence effort. Although too much duplication would be pointless, some may be necessary. The more the Europeans decide to depend on the Alliance's assets, the more they need to have assets of their own for certain key functions, so that recourse to NATO's collective assets does not lead to WEU and the European Union playing a purely superficial role. If they wish, within the framework of a common foreign and security policy, fully to exercise effective politico-military responsibilities, the WEU member states must provide themselves with, for example, military planning and intelligence facilities; they must strengthen their logistics capabilities, and develop the European armaments industry.[62]

In addition, major U.S. allies and nonaligned Western friends could supply many of the officers and other experts needed at the training centers discussed above. Such individuals might also be consultants to specific missions, particularly those using the equipment from the stocks proposed above.

Financial Issues and Assessments

UN peace operations would be greatly aided if U.S. payments were brought more consistently and promptly in line with the country's formal obligations. They would also be aided if the Pentagon were given authority to shift funds to operating accounts late in the year if its support of unexpected peace operations should drive up costs.

Ideally, the military would be provided a contingency fund of at least modest size that would be intended to fund peace operations and any related activities in their early stages. Were it roughly $1 billion a year, any large-scale U.S. peacekeeping, peace enforcement, or combat involvement would still require additional funds, which means that the president would still need to consult with Congress and the American people for difficult operations. And Congress would retain the power to cut off funds for a specific operation, as it did in a fashion for the case of Somalia, as a constraint on executive action.[63]

In addition, the United States should no longer wait until near the end of a calendar year to pay its accumulated UN dues for that year. Congress should consider appropriating, in advance, its best estimate of what the next year's costs might be. It could still wield some control over those funds, even requiring majority votes in both houses of Congress to release them for any new or expanded operations. But at least U.S. fiscal planning would be brought into closer line with what the country and the international community are calling on peacekeepers to do in the post–cold war era.[64] (Were the United States to pay at least part of the costs of individual missions promptly, the proposal put forth in the 104th Congress to reduce contributions by the anticipated dollar value of official U.S. support for UN activities might be acceptable. Otherwise, the United States would be demanding an immediate reimbursement when its late payments to the United Nations have handicapped that organization's ability to make timely reimbursements.)

Recent levels of U.S. financial contributions to UN peacekeeping may prove sufficient for the future. Those levels have been substantial: $1.1 billion and $600 million for 1994 and 1995, respectively. Costs would decline further if, as Congress, the president, and a number of independent U.S. analysts have all concluded in the last two years or so, the U.S. peacekeeping assessment rate of 32 percent were reduced to its standard UN assessment rate of 25 percent. The logic behind charging the permanent members of the Security Council more for peace operations, if ever valid, no longer is so at a time when all the world's countries share an interest in a peaceful international environment.[65] Charging the United States 25 percent of a $4 billion annual total cost would limit U.S. payments to $1 billion a year, comparable to actual 1994 assessments.

Other Financial Issues

The UN's member states might also consider providing some temporary financial relief to countries that neighbor a target of UN sanctions and are unduly burdened by those sanctions (through no fault of their own). Although of mixed effectiveness, enforced sanctions are an important component of certain UN operations and provide some leverage and deterrence. Making them work as efficiently as possible, while still no guarantee of success, is thus a worthy goal of policymakers. If the neighbors of a country subject to sanctions are highly dependent on trade with that country, as, for example, Jordan was with Iraq in 1990 and several neighbors of Yugoslavia are with that country, providing a financial cushion might help induce them to provide greater cooperation with the enforcement of sanctions.

Providing full compensation might not be practical. In addition, since countries could seek new trading partners or change their own internal economic patterns to some extent, it also might not be necessary. But to help countries adapt to the loss of perhaps billions of dollars a year in trade, temporary aid on the order of several hundred millions of dollars could be appropriate.[66]

It might be best not to overburden the official UN financial circuitry with the flow of those funds. In any case, it would be useful to coordinate any such financial assistance with the World Bank and particularly the International Monetary Fund, which have experience in cushioning economic shocks to a number of countries. They are also current on the overall status of finances, external assistance, and macroeconomics in the countries of interest.

Two other financial needs related to conflict resolution more generally concern funding for refugees and efforts to help countries reconstruct their economies and societies after protracted wars. Returning refugee per capita funding to its 1980 level would entail an added U.S. contribution of some $300 million a year. Substantial additional funding may also be needed to help internally displaced individuals, who now number almost as many as the 25 million refugees fitting the traditional meaning of the word.

Providing "peace funds," as suggested by the Overseas Development Council in Washington, as inducements to peace and a means to hasten postconflict economic reconstruction efforts might entail U.S. funds of roughly $1 billion a year. When coupled with funds from other countries, as well as loans from the international financial institutions, such sums would allow stimulus and reconstruction packages comparable to those for Haiti and the Gaza Strip–Jericho region for several countries at once. For example, if it were somehow possible to stop their conflicts over the next few years, aid might be provided to countries such as Afghanistan, Sudan, Liberia, Azerbaijan, and Tajikistan.[67] Doing so would help give soldiers more of a stake in peace and help political leaders establish the type of national consensus needed to effect it.[68]

The combined result of all these policies—more explicit planning for peace operations in the U.S. military, greater efforts to enhance other countries' abilities to contribute competently to peace operations, and economic steps to improve the enforcement of UN resolutions and help end conflict—would be much more than a symbolic approbation of multilateralism. It would help develop a complete toolkit to contain the worst excesses of civil conflict and help countries move beyond war. Peace operations would not be undertaken to assuage the collective international conscience, but to strengthen and enhance legal order, human rights, and environmentally sustainable development around the world.

Notes

1. For one cataloguing of the continuity in a number of global conflicts, see Carter Center, *1991–1992 State of World Conflict Report* (Atlanta, Ga.: Emory University, 1992), pp. 16–18.

2. "The Uses of Military Power," remarks by Secretary of Defense Caspar W. Weinberger to the National Press Club, Washington, November 28, 1984.

3. See, for example, Steven Greenhouse, "Gingrich Is Urging a Tougher Policy on Bosnia's Serbs," *New York Times*, December 5, 1994, p. 1.

4. U.S. Air Force, "Air Mobility Update: October 1994," pp. 16, 23.

5. For a similar view, see Richard N. Haass, *Intervention: The Use of American Military Force in the Post-Cold War World* (Washington: Carnegie Endowment, 1994); for a somewhat different opinion, see statement of Ernest R. May in *The Use of Force in the Post-Cold War Era*, Hearings before the House Committee on Armed Services, 103 Cong. 1 sess. (Government Printing Office, 1993), pp. 9–15.

6. Indeed, the military, like many organizations dealing with dangerous machinery, endures casualties simply by remaining ready to do its job; fatalities from training and other routine activities typically number 100 to 200 annually in peacetime.

7. For a useful discussion of some of the criteria by which the United States should judge whether or not to try to help solve a complex humanitarian crisis that involves combat, see Andrew S. Natsios, "Food through Force: Humanitarian Intervention and U.S. Policy," *Washington Quarterly*, vol. 17 (Winter 1994), pp. 129–44.

8. For similar views, see Haass, *Intervention*, pp. 1–18, 67–100; and Francis M. Deng, *Protecting the Dispossessed* (Brookings, 1993), pp. 133–40.

9. See Jeane J. Kirkpatrick and Allan Gerson, "The Reagan Doctrine, Human Rights, and International Law," in *Right v. Might: International Law and the Use of Force* (New York: Council on Foreign Relations, 1989), p. 32; Michael Walzer, *Just and Unjust Wars* (Basic Books, 1977), pp. 86, 108; Morton H. Halperin and David J. Scheffer with Patricia L. Small, *Self-Determination in the New World Order* (Washington: Carnegie Endowment, 1992); Tom J. Farer, "A Paradigm of Legitimate Intervention," in Lori Fisler Damrosch, ed., *Enforcing Restraint* (New York: Council on Foreign Relations, 1993), pp. 316–47; Boutros Boutros-Ghali, *An Agenda for Peace* (New York: United Nations, 1992), p. 8; and *Amnesty International Handbook* (New York: Amnesty International USA, 1991), pp. 11–13.

10. For a clear review of much of the last two decades, see John D. Goetke and William F. Morgan, *Review of Surface Ship Presence in Major Deployment Hubs— 1976–1982* (Alexandria, Va.: Center for Naval Analyses, 1994).

11. Department of Defense, *Defense Almanac 1994* (GPO, 1994), p. 26.

12. As discussed in more detail below, there are increasing numbers of important individuals within the Department of Defense making such arguments. See Steven Watkins, "Fogleman: Instability Is Ending," *Air Force Times*, January 23, 1995, p. 4; and "General Sheehan Advocates Shorter Deployments to Match Requirements," *Inside the Navy*, January 30, 1995, p. 1.

13. For a good discussion, see William W. Kaufmann, *A Thoroughly Efficient Navy* (Brookings, 1987), pp. 117–23.

14. Adam B. Siegel, *U.S. Navy Crisis Response Activity, 1946–1989: Preliminary Report* (Alexandria, Va.: Center for Naval Analyses, 1989), pp. 4–13; and Barry M. Blechman and Stephen S. Kaplan, *Force without War: U.S. Armed Forces as a Political Instrument* (Brookings, 1978), pp. 43–50.

15. Ronald O'Rourke, "Naval Forward Deployments and the Size of the Navy," Congressional Research Service, November 13, 1992, pp. 13–23.

16. For a good explanation of the complexities such situations pose for U.S. force planners, see Thomas L. McNaugher, *Arms and Oil: U.S. Military Strategy and the Persian Gulf* (Brookings, 1985).

17. Congressional Budget Office, *U.S. Naval Forces: The Peacetime Presence Mission* (December 1978), pp. 48–63.

18. Siegel, *U.S. Navy Crisis Response Activity*; and Blechman and Kaplan, *Force without War*.

19. See, for example, Thomas Schelling, *Arms and Influence* (Yale University Press, 1966); and Robert Jervis, *The Illogic of American Nuclear Strategy* (Cornell University Press, 1984).

20. See "Air Force to Re-Submit Presence Paper If Navy Cannot Disprove Its Findings," *Inside the Pentagon*, December 1, 1994, p. 1.

21. See, for example, "U.S. Sends Force to Protect U.N. Somalia Evacuation," *Washington Post*, January 11, 1995, p. A13.

22. See Adam B. Siegel, *The Use of Naval Forces in the Post-War Era: U.S. Navy and U.S. Marine Corps Crisis Response Activity, 1946–1990* (Alexandria, Va.: Center for Naval Analyses, 1991), pp. 39–52.

23. "General Sheehan Advocates Shorter Deployments to Match Requirements."

24. William F. Morgan, *Rotate Crews, Not Ships* (Alexandria, Va.: Center for Naval Analyses, June 1994), pp. 1–9; and William F. Morgan, *The Navy's Deployment Arithmetic—Can It Add Up to a Larger Navy?* (Alexandria, Va.: Center for Naval Analyses, August 1994), pp. 14–15.

25. Department of the Navy, *1994 Posture Statement* (1994), pp. 7, 17.

26. Goetke and Morgan, *Review of Surface Ship Presence in Major Deployment Hubs*, p. 34.

27. Secretary of Defense Les Aspin, *Report on the Bottom-Up Review* (October 1993), pp. 56–57.

28. Ronald O'Rourke, "Navy Seawolf and Centurion Attack Submarine Programs: Issues for Congress," Congressional Research Service, 1991, p. 9; and Michael E. O'Hanlon, *The Art of War in the Age of Peace* (Westport, Conn.: Praeger, 1992), pp. 41–42.

29. O'Hanlon, *Art of War in the Age of Peace*, p. 69.

30. See Michael A. Dornheim, "Fogleman to Stress 'Stability' after Deep Cuts," *Aviation Week and Space Technology,* November 7, 1994, p. 28; and Eric Schmitt, "For Better Troop Living, $2.7 Billion Is Shifted from Weapons," *New York Times*, November 11, 1994, p. A24.

31. Julie Bird, "A Time for Bold Tactics: Wing Commander to Perry: Stress Is Worsening," *Air Force Times*, October 17, 1994, p. 4.

32. See Inspector General, Department of Defense, *Catalog of Peace Operations Training Activities* (September 1994); and Barry M. Blechman and J. Matthew Vaccaro, *Training for Peacekeeping: The United Nations' Role*, Report 12 (Washington: Henry L. Stimson Center, July 1994).

33. For a description of the types of skills—such as reconnaissance, rapid deployment, helicopter assault, convoy reinforcement, and small-arms fire—most important in the ill-fated battle in Mogadishu in October 1993, see Rick Atkinson, "The Raid That Went Wrong," *Washington Post*, January 30, 1994, p. A1; Atkinson, "Night of a Thousand Casualties," *Washington Post*, January 31, 1994, p. A1; and Tony Capaccio, "Lack of Armor Didn't Lead to Ranger Deaths: Commander," *Defense Week*, January 31, 1994, p. 1.

34. A. M. Gray, Commandant of the Marine Corps, *Warfighting* (Department of the Navy, 1989), p. 22.

35. See statements of Ernest R. May and Barry R. Posen in *The Use of Force in the Post-Cold War Era*, Hearings, pp. 4–15.

36. For a somewhat different view about the suitability of standard U.S. forces for peace operations and lower-intensity conflict, see Bob Shacochis, "Our Two Armies in Haiti," *New York Times*, January 8, 1995, p. E19.

37. Aspin, *Report on the Bottom-Up Review*, pp. 22–23.

38. See, for example, Department of the Army, *FM 100-5: Operations* (June 1993), p. 2-22.

39. President Clinton expressed such views in a September 1993 speech before the United Nations General Assembly and made them official administration policy in a Presidential Decision Directive; see White House, "The Clinton Administration's Policy on Reforming Multilateral Peace Operations," May 1994. For another good example of such views, see Senator John McCain, "The Proper United States Role in Peacemaking," in Dennis J. Quinn, ed., *Peace Support Operations and the U.S. Military* (Washington: National Defense University Press, 1994), pp. 85–92.

40. Carter Center, *1991–1992 State of World Conflict Report*, pp. 16–18.

41. Les Aspin, Secretary of Defense, *Annual Report to the President and the Congress* (January 1994), p. 69.

42. In recent congressional testimony, the director of the CIA stated that some thirty places around the world showed the potential to erupt into violence. See R. James Woolsey, director of central intelligence, statement to the Senate Select Committee on Intelligence, January 10, 1995, p. 14. For a cataloguing of some sixty

disputes over territory or borders (many of which have not precipitated conflict, at least not yet), see Karin von Hippel, "The Resurgence of Nationalism and Its Implications," *Washington Quarterly*, vol. 17 (Autumn 1994), pp. 192–94.

43. Aspin, *Annual Report to the President and the Congress*, pp. 68–69.

44. For a discussion of the likely size, structure, and duration of a NATO effort to extract peacekeepers from Bosnia, see Rick Atkinson, "NATO Withdrawal Plan for Bosnia Still in Works," *Washington Post*, December 16, 1994, p. A48.

45. Department of Defense, *Defense Almanac 1994*, Issue 5 (GPO, 1994), p. 16.

46. United Nations Department of Public Information, *United Nations Peace-Keeping Operations Information Notes*, Update 2 (October 1993), pp. 64–69, and Update (May 1994), pp. 82–83, 169–73.

47. See Blechman and Vaccaro, *Training for Peacekeeping*, pp. A-1–A-6.

48. See, for example, "U.S. Considers Ghana Equipment Requests for Rwanda Operation," *Inside the Pentagon*, August 4, 1994, p. 2. UN officials also have been frustrated in their subsequent efforts to establish a peacekeeping force for the Rwandan refugee camps in Zaire in order to prevent a further phase of the war. See Raymond Bonner, "Rwanda Faces New War unless International Force Is Sent, UN Aides Say," *New York Times*, November 6, 1994, p. A12; and Julia Preston, "Force to Aid Rwandans Abandoned," *Washington Post*, January 24, 1995, p. A12.

49. Carter Center, *1991–1992 State of World Conflict Report*, p. 16.

50. See Giovanni de Briganti, "South Africa Shies Away from Lead Peacekeeping Roles," *Defense News*, November 28–December 4, 1994, p. 14.

51. Julia Preston, "UN Aide Proposes Rapid-Reaction Unit," *Washington Post*, January 6, 1995, p. A23.

52. See William J. Durch and Barry M. Blechman, *Keeping the Peace: The United Nations in the Emerging World Order* (Washington: Henry L. Stimson Center, 1992), pp. 96–97, 106–07.

53. See, for example, Julia Preston, "Waste in Somalia Typifies Failings of UN Management," *Washington Post*, January 3, 1995, p. 11.

54. See the comments of Bill Durch of the Henry Stimson Center, quoted in Sharon Denny and Jason Glashow, "UN Leaders Revisit Standing Brigade Concept," *Defense News*, October 24–30, 1994, p. 4.

55. For an expression of what one key senator sees as the appropriate limits of U.S. involvement in peacekeeping operations, see McCain, "The Proper United States Role in Peacemaking."

56. For a pessimistic outlook about such matters, see R. Jeffrey Smith, "Demand for Humanitarian Aid May Skyrocket," *Washington Post*, December 17, 1994, p. A22.

57. The author thanks William Myers for assistance with this calculation.

58. Another estimate, this one for just the training mission, can be made by scaling from the marginal cost of training a brigade-sized force at the U.S. Army training center in Hohenfels, Germany—roughly $5 million per brigade. Adding in transportation and per diem costs might double this figure, meaning that thirty brigades would train for $300 million. See statement of Edward L. Warner III, assistant secretary of defense for strategy, requirements, and resources, before the Subcommittee on Oversight and Investigation of the House Armed Services Committee, in *Peacekeeping Budget, Plans, and Actions*, H. Rept. 103-46, 103 Cong. 2 sess. (GPO, 1994), p. 11.

59. Durch and Blechman, *Keeping the Peace*, pp. 89–91.

60. For documentation of their efforts, see Ministers of Defense of Denmark,

Finland, Norway, and Sweden, *Nordic UN Stand-By Forces*, 4th ed. (Helsinki: Tryckericentralen Ab, 1993).

61. See Klaus Kinkel, minister of foreign affairs, Germany, "Peacekeeping Missions: Germany Can Now Play Its Part," *NATO Review*, vol. 42 (October 1994), p. 3.

62. Jean-Marie Guehenno, "France and the WEU," *NATO Review*, vol. 42 (October 1994), p. 12.

63. See William Matthews, "Perry Seeks Missions Funds," *Army Times*, January 9, 1994, p. 16.

64. For ideas along these lines, see Durch and Blechman, *Keeping the Peace*, pp. 62–64, 95–96; and Shijuro Ogata, Paul Volcker, and others, *Financing an Effective United Nations: A Report of the Independent Advisory Group on U.N. Financing* (New York: Ford Foundation, 1993).

65. Durch and Blechman, *Keeping the Peace*, p. vi.; and Ogata, Volcker, and others, *Financing an Effective United Nations*, p. 26.

66. Boutros-Ghali, *An Agenda for Peace*, p. 24; and Congressional Budget Office, *Enhancing U.S. Security through Foreign Aid* (April 1994), pp. 36–37.

67. See Anthony Lake and others, *After the Wars* (Washington: Overseas Development Council, 1990), pp. 14–41; John W. Sewell and Peter M. Storm, *Challenges and Priorities in the 1990s: An Alternative U.S. International Affairs Budget, FY 1993* (Washington: Overseas Development Council, 1992), pp. 31–33; and CBO, *Enhancing U.S. Security through Foreign Aid*, pp. 58–59.

68. Such a need has recently been witnessed in the Gaza Strip and Jericho region; see, for example, Clyde Haberman, "Arafat Aide Appeals to Israel and Other Nations for Help," *New York Times*, November 21, 1994.

CHAPTER FIVE

NUCLEAR WEAPONS

THE UNITED STATES decided to develop the nuclear weapon in response to fears that Nazi Germany might acquire one first and used it in a global conventional war being fought against two major industrial powers. It developed the thermonuclear weapon in response to fears of a highly ideological, ruthless, and expansionary Soviet empire that advocated global revolution. And the United States built up huge arsenals in the face of an unprecedented Soviet conventional and nuclear militarization.

Today, by contrast, aggression by the great powers is not the primary concern of the United States. It must worry instead about the proliferation of nuclear weapons to smaller countries or subnational groups that may be radicalized or ruthless like Stalin's Soviet Union. Such dangers, while markedly different from those of the cold war, are also severe—particularly in light of widespread political instability in many parts of the world that is exacerbated by rapidly growing populations and the absence of sustainable economic growth and basic human rights. In fifty short years the basic nuclear facts of life have changed drastically.

Despite widespread recognition of the dangers of proliferation, a forceful agenda for reducing nuclear danger is only half-formed in current American foreign policy. Meanwhile, stagnation in strategic arms control allows past patterns of thinking to survive, through sheer inertia, longer than they should. In the post–cold war context, unlike in previous periods, the United States has much more to lose than to gain from nuclear weapons. There is a substantial danger that too many nuclear weapons will be retained and that national security policies of the present nuclear powers will emphasize nuclear deterrence so much that opportunities to delegitimize those weapons will be forsaken.

In this strategic environment, moreover, the debate over missile defenses has become divorced from basic precepts of deterrence and arms

control theory. Traditional nuclear warfighting doctrines coexist with a
new enthusiasm for missile defenses. But to deploy large-scale defenses
without a strategy for adopting a less offensive mind-set on nuclear deterrence is a likely prescription for a renewed arms race—and a substantial worsening of the U.S.-Russian relationship.[1]

Occasional words about the benefits of having nuclear weapons available for regional conflict, in drafts of Air Force working papers or comments of high-level military officials or other semiofficial forms, legitimize
rather than delegitimize the bomb—and other countries are hardly failing
to notice.[2] During the era of U.S.-Soviet confrontation, the purpose of
nuclear weapons was to deter their use by others and to ensure the
integrity and sovereignty of the United States and allies deemed vital to
long-term U.S. national security. Preserving unfettered access to Persian
Gulf oil or some other significant, yet limited, national goal hardly qual-
ifies as comparable in importance; and the U.S. ability to preserve that
access without being the first to resort to weapons of mass destruction is
hardly in doubt.

An Alternative Nuclear Doctrine

The United States need not await START II ratification, much less
full implementation, to advance a different nuclear doctrine and accompanying set of offensive and defensive forces. The alternative nuclear
policy can be grounded in the idea that nuclear weapons have only one
acceptable mission in current U.S. military strategy: deterring the use of
weapons of mass destruction by threat of retribution. It would take a
major metamorphosis in international power balances for nuclear weapons to be required for their earlier purpose of deterring conventional
invasion of vulnerable allies—but even that purpose could be served by
a much different and more minimalist nuclear posture.

Such a philosophy would argue for much smaller arsenals and a less
ambitious plan for the Department of Energy's nuclear weapons research, development, and testing program. It would not necessarily rule
out a modest strategic defense system, but would permit such a system
only to the extent it did not risk causing an offense-defense arms race.

Another key element of such a philosophy is a nuclear no-first-use
doctrine. Such a pledge should not unduly worry conservatives on defense
matters. Other countries understand that in a worst-case scenario, where

a given state's very existence or basic well-being is at risk, preexisting pledges of no-first-use should not necessarily be viewed as entirely absolute or irrevocable. Those pledges have more to do with how militaries and security policymakers do their planning, training, and initial reacting to any crises or conflicts that may occur. They are not equivalent to unilateral disarmament in ultimate effect and thus should not be viewed as such.

The potential utility of employing warheads for nonproliferation purposes—penetrating deep underground concrete bunkers in pursuit of another country's nuclear forces, for example—might seem an important mission that would invalidate the no-first-use idea. But it is much more likely that conventional earth-penetrating and concrete-penetrating munitions could be used against any such targets; that U.S. intelligence would not have any idea of where such nuclear weapons were, making attack impossible anyway; or that the site would be sufficiently near a city that using nuclear weapons against it, particularly in a preemptive mode, would be considered morally and politically unacceptable. In addition, a nuclear warhead capable of performing such a mission could not be developed without testing. Thus any benefit from a preemptive U.S. strike capability could well be exceeded by the likely harm to nuclear nonproliferation efforts—in particular, the prospects for achieving and sustaining a comprehensive test ban, which would do much to reduce the chances other countries could develop thermonuclear weapons or missile-mounted nuclear weapons.[3]

A decision to abandon pursuit of long-term U.S. nuclear advantage and the threat of a first strike would go against cold war thinking. It could be expected to concern many of those who worry, for example, about a failure of reform in Russia or a hegemonically ascendant China. But it is precisely such concerns that the United States should now consider viewing in a new light.

Nuclear superiority, when possessed by the United States, may have conferred some slight advantages during cold war crises. But classic deterrence theory suggests that it was much more the political willingness to draw lines and take risks that determined outcomes in such settings.[4] On balance, the deterrent benefit of nuclear weapons was rather modest—the clearest and simplest proof being that the Soviet Union, China, and some of their allies began wars of aggression or occupations during a period of American nuclear monopoly and overwhelming superiority. Taking nuclear risks may or may not have been appropriate during the global ideological struggle between East and West. But it does not seem appropriate for what are likely to be more specific and limited contests with future great powers over limited amounts of territory or access to specific resources, generally in their own proximity. Economic deterrence would seem more appropriate for such stakes.[5]

Someday, it may be possible and desirable to pursue international control of nuclear weapons.[6] But the United Nations at present is a long way from having either the political decisionmaking processes or the technical capabilities to manage the world's ultimate military deterrent. In addition, the world is a long way from developing and manifesting the type of international security regime that would probably be required to convince certain countries that they did not need nuclear weapons.[7] However, a much-revised nuclear force structure and doctrine should be implemented without further delay. Failing to do so may well imperil rigorous enforcement and sustainment of the nuclear Non-Proliferation Treaty regime and other international efforts to stanch proliferation and punish transgressors.[8]

An Alternative Nuclear Force

Translating this type of doctrine into an actual force involves not only strategic offensive forces but also strategic and theater defenses, Department of Energy nuclear warhead work, and communications and intelligence.

Offensive Nuclear Forces

A first step to further reductions would not itself entail warhead cuts, given the need to do so through negotiation, but would deploy U.S. warheads more economically in the interim before further negotiated cuts. Rather than retain 14 Trident submarines, 450 to 500 Minuteman III missiles, and a nuclear bomber force of 66 B-52s and 20 B-2s, as the administration envisions, an alternative that could be implemented right away would make do with 9 Trident submarines and 100 Minuteman III missiles (see table 5-1). The first cut in platforms would be compensated for by deploying each D5 or Trident II missile with its full complement of eight warheads, as originally intended when the missile was designed, rather than the five warheads now planned. The second would be bal-

Table 5-1. An Alternative Defense Posture for Nuclear Forces

Type of program or unit	BUR	Alternative
Minuteman III ICBMs	450–500	100
Trident submarines	14	9
Deployed submarine-launched missiles	336	216
D5 submarine-launched missiles	432	337
DOE nuclear weapons research, development, and testing	$1.6 billion/year	$1.3 billion/year
DOE nuclear weapons stockpile support	$1.6 billion/year	$1.4 billion/year
Communications	$20 billion/year	$19 billion/year
Intelligence	$28 billion/year	$26 billion/year
Warheads	5,000 or more	1,000–3,500

anced either by restoring full warhead loadings—some 20 cruise missiles—to the B-52 fleet or by retaining the B-1 bomber as a dual-purpose platform rather than dedicating it exclusively to conventional weapons missions. In addition to annual operating cost reductions of more than $1 billion a year for the smaller Minuteman force and Trident force, this approach would permit acquisition savings: the D5 missile program could be terminated immediately, with net savings of about a billion dollars a year for the rest of the decade, and the $5 billion Minuteman III guidance upgrade program could be scaled back to simply a maintenance effort.[9]

A second step would have Russia and the United States proceed quickly to a START III framework that allowed each country 1,000 deployed strategic warheads of types of its own choosing (multiple-warhead ICBMs would remain banned, as they are under START II). Indeed, beginning to discuss or even promote the idea soon could aid START II's prospects. Many Russians are concerned about the sincerity of U.S. arms control efforts as reflected in the START II Treaty because that treaty's treatment of multiple-warhead ICBMs works somewhat against Russian interests, and ratification may be in jeopardy as a result.[10] Preferably, the other declared nuclear powers could simultaneously be convinced to provide politically binding commitments to freeze their nuclear arsenals at (or below) their current levels; in such a form, a START III framework seems consistent with President Yeltsin's September 1994 speech to the UN General Assembly.[11] The alert levels of U.S. and Russian arsenals should also be lowered. Doing so safely would be facilitated by keeping

Table 5-2. Illustrative Nuclear Target Sets

Target category	Approximate number of aimpoints[a]
Targets associated with conventional military forces	
Airfields (fixed-wing aircraft and helicopters)	30–40
Marshaling yards	30 or more
Major supply depots (front level and above)	10
Command and control centers (army levels and above)	25 or more
Fixed ammunition storage sites	20–30
Major petroleum, oil, and lubricants pipelines	10–15
Bridges, other major choke points	50
Targets associated with industry	
Molybdenum, nickel, magnesium	1
Titanium	2
Lead	4
Copper	12
Aluminum	17
Steel	36
Petroleum	70

Source: Congressional Budget Office, *The START Treaty and Beyond* (October 1991), pp. 22–24.

a. The information in this table is based primarily on data for Russian industry and forces but should be useful for illustrative purposes for other large countries' assets as well.

at least some land-based missiles in silos (some would survive any first strike even if not on alert) and perhaps by a different approach to ballistic missile submarine patrols.[12]

Arsenals with 1,000 warheads each would seem to be quite ample. Indeed, China, Britain, France, and Israel seem comfortable owning arsenals with a few hundred warheads each. Deterring the use of nuclear weapons by other countries can probably be satisfied by no more than tens of survivable warheads, as the likes of Bernard Brodie, Thomas Schelling, McGeorge Bundy, and Herbert York have argued. Using nuclear weapons as last-resort tools to massively disrupt an all-out conventional invasion by a major power might require on the order of 100 to 400 weapons against the major depots, transportation nodes, war industries, marshaling points, and related nodes of a conventional military operation (see table 5-2).[13] Such a use of weapons could cause casualties exceeding the scale of what occurred in the world wars, however, meaning that the attacks would best be seen as entering the realm of terror.[14] Viewing them as countermilitary at that point would make little sense.

Arsenals with 1,000 warheads would, depending on the exact disposition of forces and the way weapons performed, provide second-strike capabilities with numbers of warheads in the low to mid-hundreds. Submarines deployed at sea, particularly American vessels but probably at least some Russian vessels, would be likely to elude any attack. For the United States, survivable submarine warheads might represent 30 percent to 60 percent of the country's initial submarine force. Warheads based in missile silos would have a probability of roughly 5 percent to 25 percent of surviving attack, depending on assumptions about the accuracy of warheads attacking them and other factors. Bombers on runway alert at inland bases would generally survive, at least the first few to leave a given base after warning of an attack was received; those not on alert would almost certainly not survive.

Thus a completely unexpected surprise attack against forces on low alert might destroy as much as 90 percent of a 1,000-warhead U.S. force evenly divided among ICBM, SLBM, and bomber warheads—that is, almost all weapons except those on whatever fraction of the submarine force was deployed at sea at the time. More likely, accounting for the difficulties in attacking missile silo fields with multiple warheads, it would destroy perhaps 80 percent of the notional 1,000-warhead force. An all-out first strike during a crisis, when more submarines could be expected to be at sea and at least some bombers would be on runway alert, would destroy perhaps half of an adversary's force (the United States might, however, be able to destroy a somewhat higher fraction of Russian forces by trailing its ballistic missile submarines).[15]

Theater and Strategic Missile Defenses

There are two main dimensions to the problem of missile defenses: technological feasibility and political or arms control desirability. On both, in contrast to the days of heated superpower arms competition, moderate positions seem called for in the post–cold war context. But any thought about deploying a defense larger than allowed by the ABM Treaty should be pursued only if targeting procedures, doctrines, and the sizes of arsenals are revised fundamentally to reflect a more minimalist role for nuclear weapons. Otherwise, the risk of recreating an arms race would be too high to justify the likely benefit.

Beginning with the issue of theater defenses, a number of efforts are currently well under way. They include the Patriot advanced capability-3 system using the extended-range interceptor as a "hit-to-kill" last stage, the theater high altitude area defense system for coverage of broader land areas, and the ship-based standard missile program using the Aegis radar capabilities of cruisers and destroyers. Future programs are intended to include a wider- and higher-range sea-based missile system, the corps surface-to-air missile system for short-range air defense of ground troops, and perhaps boost-phase intercept technologies mounted on tactical combat aircraft.

Because of improvements in sensors and software, it is not clear that the usefulness of all such systems would be confined to defending against only theater or shorter-range missiles. Once their ability to work in tandem with a ground-based control center was established against an object moving at four or five kilometers per second, these systems might have the potential to be effective against a strategic reentry vehicle moving at seven kilometers per second. However, the defending country probably would not have confidence in something not tested for such a purpose, nor could the potential attacking country be sure it would not work. This explains the current disagreements in U.S.-Russian discussions on the issue.

It will be difficult to construct a reliable technical cutoff—such as a threshold based on the speed of the incoming warhead, the speed of the outgoing interceptor missile, or the range of that missile—in such a way that a theater system tested below that cutoff will be incapable of strategic missile defense. Although such limits could be useful, limits on numbers of theater-defense interceptor missiles would be a useful adjunct.

Defending the fifty largest U.S. cities against a second-strike attack of 200 warheads, for example, might require only 300 to 500 interceptors if the attacker would be so cooperative as to distribute the attack in precise tandem with the geographic distribution of the defensive deployment. But an attacker could concentrate its barrage of warheads against only five or ten of those cities, perhaps not destroying all of the country's largest cities but killing millions of people. (Alternatively, it could concentrate on U.S. conventional military facilities.) To defeat such a concentrated attack, a defender would need 1,500 or more interceptor missiles (assuming an intercept probability of roughly 0.7 and long-range interceptors capable of being used in "shoot-look-shoot" mode). Accepting a limit of perhaps 1,500 medium- and long-range theater defense missiles would, according to this perspective, help address the concern that highly capable next-generation theater defense systems could constitute a latent strategic defense capability. At the same time, such a limit would still permit a substantial defensive capability against a regional foe.[16]

Concerning strategic missile defenses, a number of points are worth making. Large-scale missile defense against a determined adversary remains a highly dubious proposition. A substantial number of penetrating warheads could be expected because of the sheer enormity of any likely exchange and the attacker's innate ability to concentrate attack against certain parts of a defense and to use sophisticated countermeasures to overwhelm sensors.

Defense against a smaller nuclear power is much more feasible, although it is also important not to overstate the likelihood of achieving a highly reliable leakproof shield. Sensors have improved sufficiently to allow discrimination between real warheads and simple decoys, at least within the atmosphere; computers and software are increasingly able to handle the amounts of data associated with a limited attack; and interceptor rockets may no longer require nuclear warheads to provide a high probability of intercept. Still, such advanced integrated defense systems have not yet been reliably demonstrated; moreover, means other than normal ballistic missile delivery—use of sophisticated decoys, cruise missiles, commercial ships or planes, or prior planting of nuclear devices in cities—generally would not be negated by a missile defense system.

As long as the nuclear superpowers view deterrence as requiring a detailed nuclear warplan involving hundreds or thousands of weapons, deploying anything more than very small defenses will remain dangerous to arms control and to security in any future crisis. If Russia retained highly capable offensive weapons while developing large-scale defenses, the United States would not find that situation consistent with its prevailing view of what its own deterrent force must be capable of achieving. By the same token, Russia could not be expected to accept a similar U.S. approach unless it were willing to accept strategic inferiority. In point of fact, however, Russia seems very unlikely to accept strategic nuclear inferiority—particularly at a time when talk of NATO expansion increases the potential array of conventional forces that could be directed against it and when U.S. nuclear counterforce strategy has not been renounced.

The original ABM Treaty permitted up to 200 interceptors at two sites. That number of strategic interceptor missiles might be a reasonable number to permit, although it might be appropriate to allow them at more than the two sites envisioned under that framework. Such an approach would of course require modification of the ABM Treaty. If the United States and Russia someday both adopted a more minimalist type of nuclear deterrence doctrine that placed less emphasis on destroying a large target set or on ensuring thorough societal destruction, further relaxation of the ABM Treaty might be considered.[17] For example, something like the ground-based element of the Bush administration's GPALS proposal—750 interceptors—might be acceptable under a 1,000-warhead START III framework. An attacker could still saturate, and thus defeat, such a defense in one or two geographic regions even in a second strike.

Department of Energy Nuclear Weapons Work

The above-mentioned changes in nuclear weapons posture and doctrine also imply that the so-called stockpile stewardship program and the weapons production infrastructure of the Department of Energy can be scaled back. Stockpile stewardship as presently advertised seeks to preserve warhead capabilities at their previous levels. It also plans to improve the state of knowledge of nuclear warhead science in order to provide the basis for modifying or improving weapons at some future date should that be desired. Reducing such programs would send the important message that the United States does not view preservation or improvements of each and every nuclear weapons capability as a basic requirement for security. Yet the remaining program, as outlined below, would still allow the country to retain very high confidence in its basic deterrent. In a worst case, one or two classes of warheads out of six or eight might have marginally lower performance or reliability.

Under my alternative, DOE would undertake a complete shutdown of the Nevada test site, an end to the integrated nuclear weapons stewardship responsibilities of the Lawrence Livermore National Laboratory— as recently suggested by the secretary of energy's advisory panel on the future of the DOE laboratory system, or Galvin panel—and a reduction of the funding levels for cooperative research and development agreements to the 1993 level of $140 million.[18] Total savings would reach about $300 million a year. A smaller nuclear arsenal, and a decision that the arsenal could remain smaller even under pessimistic assumptions about the future of great-power relations, would allow a scaling back of the U.S. nuclear warhead production complex and additional savings of about $200 million a year.[19]

Intelligence and Communications for
Nuclear and Conventional Forces

Tied to all U.S. military forces, and indeed all of U.S. security posture, is the nearly $50 billion that the United States spends each year to obtain and distribute information critical to national security decision-making and warfighting.

It is difficult to assess the proper amount of spending on intelligence and communications technologies because of the secrecy in which such matters are shrouded. Moreover, cutbacks in this area are in many ways less pressing than those in combat forces, since there is probably less harm done in erring on the side of too much capability. Security dilemma dynamics do not enter into play as quickly, except for certain technologies directly tied to weapons systems, such as some of the sensors for strategic defense systems.

Yet there are good reasons to consider cutting this area of spending further. The annual intelligence budget is reported to have absorbed cuts of some $5 billion since the end of the cold war. But it remains above real levels of the early 1980s, when a major Soviet threat still existed. Personnel levels are continuing to decline over the decade for an aggregate planned reduction of some 23 percent from the 1990 benchmark. But overall spending levels may not decline because of the escalating costs of new intelligence-gathering systems as well as severance and retirement programs for many staff.[20] Indeed, the president's 1996 budget request reportedly calls for a steady level of spending on intelligence (though unclassified accounts do not specify if the units of denomination are current or constant dollars).

In that light, while detailed suggestions for how cuts might be made are difficult to offer, further reductions in funding seem reasonable. Planned cuts of roughly 20 percent are somewhat more than half as large as the 35 percent cuts in overall military spending occurring over the course of the 1990s. If the same ratio applied to further cuts, my suggested reductions of roughly 20 percent in force structure would produce a cut possibly approaching 10 percent in intelligence spending, or at least $2 billion annually. Some areas in which cuts seem possible include duplication in military intelligence operations at the service and command levels; duplicative gathering of basic data on military forces by the CIA and the military services; and excessive intelligence resources devoted to matters such as commerce and environmental issues for which alternative sources of information generally exist.[21]

Communications systems seem appropriate candidates for restructuring as part of a reexamination of service roles and missions. General Merrill A. McPeak suggested such an approach that would consolidate most systems under his service's control in a major paper late in 1994, when he was chief of staff of the Air Force. The Air Force's representative to the Roles and Missions Commission later estimated it held the potential to save nearly $1 billion a year.[22] Such prospective savings, and the technical feasibility of consolidating communications in that manner, are consistent with analyses by the General Accounting Office as well.[23] It is difficult to comment on those findings without conducting a technically detailed and probably classified study on military communication requirements. But with such high-level support for the idea, so much money at stake, and rapid communications so important in an era of reconnaissance-strike joint warfare, the onus is on the defenders of the status quo to prove the Air Force and GAO wrong. The sheer redundancy of existing systems, which include Air Force, Navy, and DOD-wide communications satellite networks, suggest that the reformers' arguments may well be right.

The answers about where to go next in nuclear arms control are not yet fully apparent. Major challenges include how to balance smaller offensive forces with some defensive capability and how to deal over the long term with the two-tiered system of nuclear haves and have-nots. But one thing is clear: the current START II framework, if implemented, is insufficient. All it would accomplish is to return superpower strategic nuclear forces to the place they were when the SALT process began more than twenty-five years ago. That is no mean feat, but the starting line is no place to stop. All tools that can contribute to reducing nuclear danger must be employed: offensive arms control, a truly comprehensive test ban, properly designed modest defenses, and a declaratory and doctrinal posture that delegitimizes the bomb.

Notes

1. See Freeman Dyson, *Weapons and Hope* (Harper and Row, 1984), pp. 272–85.

2. See, for example, the widely circulated, though later modified, draft paper by

Thomas C. Reed and Michael Wheeler, "The Role of Nuclear Weapons in the New World Order," U.S. Air Force, December 18, 1991, p. 15; and McGeorge Bundy, "Nuclear Weapons and the Gulf," *Foreign Affairs*, vol. 70 (Fall 1991), pp. 83–94. See also Patrick E. Tyler, "China Warns against 'Star Wars' Shield for U.S. Forces in Asia," *New York Times*, February 18, 1995, p. 4.

3. That a comprehensive test ban treaty would make it difficult for other countries to develop thermonuclear weapons or missile-delivered nuclear weapons is discussed in Congressional Budget Office, "The Bomb's Custodians," CBO Paper (July 1994), p. 3.

4. Thomas C. Schelling, *Arms and Influence* (Yale University Press, 1966).

5. Richard K. Betts, *Nuclear Blackmail and Nuclear Balance* (Brookings, 1987); see also McGeorge Bundy, *Danger and Survival* (Vintage Books, 1988), pp. 586–607; and James A. Nathan, "The Heyday of the New Strategy: The Cuban Missile Crisis and the Confirmation of Coercive Diplomacy," in James A. Nathan, ed., *The Cuban Missile Crisis Revisited* (St. Martin's Press, 1992), p. 17.

6. For examples of such ideas, see Henry L. Stimson Center, "Beyond the Nuclear Peril," Washington, 1995; and Stephen S. Rosenfeld, "New Age Nukes," *Washington Post*, February 10, 1995, p. A23.

7. For an insightful discussion of the linkage between global security regimes and nonproliferation efforts, see Roger D. Speed, *The International Control of Nuclear Weapons* (Stanford, Calif.: Center for International Security and Arms Control, June 1994), pp. 11–31.

8. Selig S. Harrison, "Zero Nuclear Weapons. Zero," *New York Times*, February 15, 1995, p. A21.

9. General Accounting Office, *ICBM Modernization: Minuteman III Guidance Replacement Program Has Not Been Adequately Justified*, NSIAD-93-181 (June 1993).

10. "Officials Predict START II Will Be Shot Down in Russian Parliament," *Inside the Pentagon*, December 22, 1994, p. 2.

11. See Fred Hiatt, "Yeltsin Arms Proposals Aimed at Russians, Historians," *Washington Post*, September 28, 1994, p. A14.

12. For a discussion of the survivability of missile silos, see Congressional Budget Office, *The START Treaty and Beyond* (October 1991), pp. 80–84, 143–65. Options for submarine alert levels can be found in Bruce G. Blair, *Global Zero Alert for Nuclear Forces* (Brookings, 1995). See also Jonathan Dean, "The Final Stage of Nuclear Arms Control," *Washington Quarterly*, vol. 17 (Autumn 1994), p. 46.

13. CBO, *The START Treaty and Beyond*, pp. 14–15; and Michael J. Mazarr and the CSIS Nuclear Strategy Study Group, *Toward A Nuclear Peace* (Washington: Center for Strategic and International Studies, June 1993), pp. viii–xii.

14. Barbara G. Levi, Frank N. von Hippel, and William H. Daugherty, "Civilian Casualties from 'Limited' Nuclear Attacks on the Soviet Union," *International Security*, vol. 12 (Winter 1987–1988), pp. 168–89.

15. CBO, *The START Treaty and Beyond*, pp. 86–87; and Congressional Budget Office, "Implementing START II," CBO Paper (March 1993), pp. 2–4, 59.

16. See Stephen Weiner, "Systems and Technology," in Ashton B. Carter and David N. Schwartz, eds., *Ballistic Missile Defense* (Brookings, 1984), pp. 63–78; and David Mosher and Raymond Hall, "The Clinton Plan for Theater Missile Defenses: Costs and Alternatives," *Arms Control Today*, vol. 24 (September 1994), pp. 15–20.

17. For a vision of future security relations consistent with this thinking, see Dyson, *Weapons and Hope*, pp. 280–81.

18. See CBO, "The Bomb's Custodians," pp. ix–xvi.

19. See Congressional Budget Office, *Reducing the Deficit: Spending and Revenue Options* (March 1994), pp. 24–25.

20. Congressional Budget Office, "Easing the Burden: Restructuring and Consolidating Defense Support Activities" (July 1994), pp. 53–66.

21. See Walter Pincus, "Senior CIA Official Criticizes Past Estimates, Urges Change in Emphasis," *Washington Post*, September 23, 1994, p. A23; CBO, "Easing the Burden," pp. 53–66; and Robert M. Gates, "A Leaner, Keener CIA," *Washington Post*, January 30, 1995, p. A15.

22. See General Merrill A. McPeak, chief of Staff of the U.S. Air Force, *Presentation to the Commission on Roles and Missions of the Armed Forces* (September 14, 1994), pp. 185–99; and Jason Glashow and Steve Weber, "USAF Promises Savings by Space Control," *Defense News*, September 26–October 2, 1994, p. 8.

23. General Accounting Office, *Military Satellite Communications: Opportunity to Save Billions of Dollars*, NSIAD-93-216 (July 1993).

CHAPTER SIX

SECURITY STRUCTURES AND DEFENSE POSTURES FOR THE TWENTY-FIRST CENTURY

IN PRESENTING AN ALTERNATIVE force structure and security doctrine, I have thus far focused on the near term, talking about a strategy for transition. This raises the obvious question of transition to what? It is beyond the scope of this book to flesh out in detail key elements of a long-term security architecture. But even a near-term defense plan must be evaluated in terms of the direction in which it tries to influence future international relations, not just by the immediate effects it has on dealing with today's problems.

Fortunately, many sensible elements of a post–cold war U.S. foreign policy are already in place. The United States continues, for example, to espouse an international trading system that should help other countries grow economically and to hold out a political model that should help them democratize. By preserving its involvement in global military alliances, the United States does much to continue giving those alliances meaning and holding them together. By remaining committed to other countries' security, it helps deter substantial territorial aggression by other powers. By strengthening its own economy through deficit reduction, continued support for basic research, and other means, it fires an engine of global economic growth and technological progress. And by promoting a number of treaties and supplier agreements to control the spread of weapons of mass destruction, while at the same time taking modest steps to reduce the role of nuclear weapons in its own security policies, the United States in conjunction with other countries is pursuing at least the rudiments of a sensible two-pronged nonproliferation policy.

But it is not enough to perpetuate such sound cold war policies. Without predicting the demise of the United States or even its decline as a world leader, it is safe to conclude that this country will not forever be able to play the role of a sole global superpower in every major industrial region of the world.[1] Indeed, it is only able to do so today because the world's other major industrial powers are its allies and because they generally share U.S. foreign policy goals. Moreover, the advantages of being a superpower accrue only if there exists a constructive U.S. vision for shaping the future global order.

This chapter considers several elements of a future vision for U.S. foreign policy, particularly the structure and functioning of alliances. One set of issues pertains to the North Atlantic Treaty Organization and another to the U.S.-Korean relationship. A third concerns U.S. relations with several principal recipients of its arms transfers not included in the other two categories, namely, Taiwan and the Arab countries of the Gulf Cooperation Council. Together, how these issues are handled will do much to determine the future character of the Western alliance and thus that alliance's relations with Russia, China, and other potential or emerging powers.

Many self-styled realists argue that the international environment of the future is likely to resemble that of the past, that war is likely to be an intractable dimension of most types of international relations, and that Russia and China in particular are likely to be adversarial. These arguments are useful cautionary warnings. But as guides to policy they can be self-fulfilling, and as predictions of what things will be they overstep any claim to being scientific or even solidly grounded in historical analysis.[2] Many realists seem to ignore, for example, the significance of the fact that the Western world appears to represent a cohesive political-economic-military bloc within which countries need not fear each other or plan against each other—a state of affairs in flat contradiction to the spirit of most traditional realist theory. Those countries have effectively established a cooperative security regime already. Being democratic, not depending for their economic well-being on new territorial acquisition, being chastened by the destructiveness of past wars, and staying appropriately fearful of the ongoing potential for war, they have reached a maturity in their relations where large-scale conflict between them seems implausible.[3]

Few realists challenge this assertion of Western cohesion, except sometimes in barely whispered residual fears about Germany or Japan. Yet they seem unwilling to believe that similarly constructive and reliable relations might be fashioned with the likes of Russia or China or think about what policy tools might improve the chances that such relations will emerge over time. Admittedly, the opportunities to impose U.S.

norms, constitutional principles, and legal procedures do not exist in those countries today in the way that they presented themselves in Germany and Japan after World War II. Nor does the presence of a traditional external threat impel these countries to band together. But the experience of working together for years through the UN Security Council and other mechanisms, together with the importance of avoiding conflict in the twenty-first century and providing for a demographically and environmentally sustainable means of global economic growth, should provide impetus and hope.

The NATO Alliance

The major military alliances of the United States in East Asia and Europe no longer have a clear Soviet threat to justify their existence. Security planners should therefore evaluate them afresh. In so doing, they should avoid assuming axiomatically that any U.S.-based alliance will be a positive force for global stability. Alliances may have been necessary to win the world wars and prevail in the cold war. But they also can be dangerous, as witnessed notably in events leading up to the outbreak of World War I. Particularly when they become instruments for preserving or expanding influence, rather than ensuring self-defense or shaping the basic character of a global power system, they can be harmful just as easily as helpful.[4]

NATO Expansion

The logic of NATO as a response to an aggressive, militarist, and heavily armed Soviet Union could hardly be doubted. But the logic of encircling an economically destitute former superpower with the richest and most capable military alliance in the world's history, and sometimes signaling intent to react forcefully to disputes that now-democratic superpower may have with its neighbors, is by contrast unlikely to appear reasonable even to fair-minded Russian democrats. Combined with other simmering issues in which the West is generally seeking to impose its will on Russia, NATO expansion could contribute to the resurgence of extreme Russian nationalism. But this argument should not be overstated; indeed, if such external developments could so easily tilt the balance of power within Russia toward dangerous extremism, advocates of NATO expansion would have a stronger case than they actually do. More likely, NATO expansion would not fundamentally change Russian foreign policy behavior, but could lead Russia to keep a military force too large for the country's economy to bear—virtually ensuring that troops charged with enforcing nuclear security, internal order, and other critical functions will be underpaid, disgruntled, and at times unprofessional.

Were NATO extended only as far as the so-called Visegrad countries— that is, Poland, Hungary, Slovakia, and the Czech Republic—it would do little to address the concerns of countries such as Ukraine that actually could have something to fear from a militarist Russian government.[5] In addition, such expansion would do little to address the type of conflict most likely to cause problems in the future Europe: not naked wars of conquest, but those blurring the distinction between civil strife and interstate conflict that grow out of contests over borders with questionable historical, ethnic, and political legitimacy.

Conversely, if NATO were instead extended to the Baltic states and Ukraine, it could do much harm. Russia might be prepared to challenge the West over a matter such as Crimea.[6] Russia still sees itself as a great power, possesses the nuclear weapons of a great power, and intends to play the role of a great power, particularly adjacent to its own borders. Raising the specter of a Western military challenge to any such potential Russian tensions with Ukraine or some other new neighbor, especially in a predeclared manner that is blind to how a crisis or conflict was caused, would be extremely unwise.

Russia is highly unlikely to return to the imperialism of its nineteenth-century past (not unlike the nineteenth-century imperialism of many countries now members of NATO). Its interests and ambitions need to be understood in modern great-power terms. In a fashion similar to that of Western powers, it now shows self-serving yet "normal" (not generally ideologically or imperialistically driven) economic and political interests in certain regions and countries.

Although there may be situations where Western pressure can play a useful role in restraining Russian ambitions, it is wrongheaded to assume that Russia or any other major power would welcome such pressure or not feel threatened militarily by it. It is also incorrect that Russia's unhappiness over such a situation implies that it necessarily remains latently or actively imperialist.[7] R. James Woolsey made precisely these points in cogent congressional testimony at the end of his tenure as head of Central Intelligence:

Let me address the question as to whether there has been a significant change in the direction of Russian foreign policy, manifested at the CSCE Summit of last December and in Russia's public comments about NATO expansion. We believe that a consensus has emerged in Moscow over the past two years for a more intense focus on Russian interests. These include: maintaining a sphere of influence in the Newly Independent States which today are home to 25 million ethnic Russians; reestablishing Russia as a key actor in Europe, the Middle East, and East Asia; and establishing a "balanced" partnership with the United States. . . .

I am not suggesting a return to a cold war with Russia—indeed, on a number of these issues we have also had disagreements with our closest allies. But it is clear that Russia is redefining its position in foreign policy, and making clear its desire to maintain a position of influence in world affairs.[8]

At a time when every permanent member of the UN Security Council exercises influence and national prerogative in ways that Washington does not like, only Russia and China are accused of being dangerous because they do so. This thereby increases the chances that further misunderstandings will occur and opportunities to advance working relationships will be missed. This antagonism also could lead Russia to attempt to keep an armed force still much too big for the financial resources available to support it, out of fear not of its immediate neighbors but of the West in general. An armed force of such excessive size and poor repair is poorly equipped to handle the absolutely essential jobs of maintaining nuclear security and preserving national cohesion. These points should concern the West far more than the remote and unlikely specter of a Russian invasion of central Europe.[9] A state of antagonism between Russia and the West also could further slow or end cooperative threat reduction through transparency over nuclear warheads and materials, destruction of excess weapons, and improved Russian export controls.[10] In addition, increasing discord in Security Council settings could be expected, which would hamstring efforts to establish better methods and ideas on when and how the United Nations should intervene to defend human rights, nuclear weapons security, and other core priorities of a cooperative global security regime.

Western policymakers might take a page from Ukraine, whose current president, Leonid Kuchma, is an opponent of rapid moves toward NATO expansion.[11] Despite having much more genuine cause for concern about Russian behavior than the West, Ukraine agreed to give up its nuclear weapons and accede to the Non-Proliferation Treaty in order to avoid nuclear warhead safety problems, extract a pledge of nonaggression from

Russia, and attempt to build a more cooperative framework for relations.[12]

No one can predict what the effects of NATO expansion would be on the course of Russian politics. But if there is anything to the argument that the Soviet Union—largely through its own fault, to be sure—had reason to begin to feel encircled and threatened in the late 1970s and 1980s by a strong Western Europe, U.S.-Chinese and Japanese-Chinese rapprochement, and the Reagan military buildup, one could expect much more serious concerns in Moscow now.[13] The justifiable level of fear in Russia is substantial, given an economically explosive China on one border, expanding and still very strong NATO on another, latent tensions over borders and minority rights with other former Soviet republics, and turmoil within the Russian republic itself. Russian military views and some recent official statements have lent credence to the idea that a number of individuals are acutely concerned about these developments.[14]

Even reasonable Russians are bound to be worried about a NATO that shows no signs of dissolution despite the end of its alleged raison d'être, occasionally suggests that Ukraine and the Baltic states might need Western military defense against Russia, and possesses overwhelming air superiority that could greatly influence ground battles within the territories of the former Soviet republics.[15] As Elaine Sciolino of the *New York Times* put it flatly and compellingly, "Although the United States and its NATO partners insist that no European nations would be prevented from eventually joining NATO . . . both NATO and Moscow know that Russia remains the perceived enemy in Europe and would be at the bottom of the list."[16]

Moreover, as former Reagan defense official Fred Iklé recently argued, the West's indecisiveness about the wisdom, value, and nature of NATO expansion flies in the face of retaining a credible core purpose for the alliance. Current thinking that NATO would not place foreign troops in the Visegrad countries, while in many ways sensible, signals a two-tiered NATO, casting into doubt the West's real willingness to defend the Czech and Slovak republics, Poland, and Hungary.[17]

Of course, it is true that Russia, or any number of other countries for that matter, could over the long term pose acute threats to neighbors. It is then that the formation of military alliances would make sense; indeed, it was precisely under such circumstances that NATO itself was formed some four decades ago. The vision of cooperative security—which in essence represents a new twist on the adage that states have no permanent allies, only permanent interests—argues that the United States should not ally against countries but only against regimes bent on conquest or ruthless rule. Russia may have political elements that cause concern in such a light, but it certainly does not now have a government or political system fitting such a fearsome mold.

If the idea of NATO expansion does ultimately prevail, much of the damage that it might cause could be mitigated by stating emphatically that the alliance sees itself largely as serving new purposes outside of Europe (see below) as well as strictly defensive purposes within Europe. [18] Also important would be acceptance of a mutual nonaggression pact, as recently proposed by Russia. It would recognize most disputes between the West and Moscow, such as those over the former Yugoslavia, Chechnya, and Iran, as normal if sometimes unfortunate disagreements between great powers rather than as signs of pending all-out confrontation, and it would revise the set of policy instruments to be used in addressing those disagreements accordingly. [19]

Redefining NATO's Purpose and Reshaping Military Forces

With or without expansion, NATO can reinvigorate itself and mitigate the concerns of neighboring countries such as Russia by transforming its raison d'être. The alliance's future purpose should be primarily to serve as a basis for military cooperation in new missions, as well as a symbol of Western cohesion that embodies the cooperative security concept. NATO provides means to coordinate some types of equipment acquisition, base assets, training and operating procedures, deployments, and any actual combat activities that may occur in the future. Without it, for example, conducting the Gulf War would have been considerably more complicated militarily. [20]

Today, the United States is doing most of the heavy lifting for the Western world's real security agenda, raising doubts as to the sustainability of the Western alliance in an era of fiscal pressures and a murky strategic threat environment. It should not be that way. The spending and troop levels of major U.S. allies, while not as great as those of the United States, are significant, exceeding $150 billion a year in aggregate among the other NATO countries and Japan. Their troops number well over 1 million in all. But U.S. allies are not particularly well set up to deploy significant combat forces to outside areas. Only the British, and to a lesser extent the French, seem likely to be significant partners, as dem-

Table 6-1. Potential Power Projection Forces of NATO Countries[a]

Country	Modern tactical combat wings (aircraft)	Modern heavy divisions (tanks)
United Kingdom	3 (300 Tornado)	2 (426 Challenger, 495 Chieftain)
France	2½ (230 Mirage 2000)	2 (1,000 AMX-30)
Germany	2 (190 Tornado)	2½ (730 Leopard 1A5, Leopard 2)
Italy	⅔ (70 Tornado)	2 (910 Leopard)
Netherlands	1½ (150 F-16)	⅔ (444 Leopard 2)
Belgium	1⅓ (133 F-16)	⅔ (334 Leopard)
Turkey	1⅓ (140 F-16)	⅔ (400 Leopard)
Spain	⅔ (70 F-18)	⅔ (280 AMX-30)
Other	2¾ (275 modern combat aircraft)	2⅓ (about 900 modern tanks)
Total	About 15	About 13

Sources: International Institute for Strategic Studies, *The Military Balance 1994-1995* (London: Brassey's, 1994), pp. 34–72; White Papers of the Ministries of Defense of Belgium, Denmark, France, Germany, and the United Kingdom; and author's estimates.

a. Excludes United States. These forces have the combat equipment necessary to be effective outside of Europe, but generally do not have the logistics support and other necessary features for such purposes.

onstrated in Desert Storm.[21] However, even there the combined contributions of those two countries was about 50,000 troops, of which a single heavy division and roughly two wings were constituted. Since that time, troop and budget cuts have reduced the likely size of any future deployment. The French-German–based Eurocorps of some 40,000 troops is due to become operational in 1995 and may provide the nucleus for future pan-European efforts to develop flexible, sizable, and mobile forces. But at least initially its size and heavy capabilities will be modest and its actual availability unproven politically.[22]

For the future, European militaries should be set up to provide at least five to seven ground divisions and a comparable number of wings of combat aircraft, as well as transport and logistics support, for any future regional conflict. They possess much of the necessary equipment (see table 6-1). By obtaining such capabilities, they could reduce the chances of backlash by the American people against perceived free riders and give further meaning to the concept of cooperative security.

U.S. Alliances in East Asia

A second important set of issues worth flagging at this point, even if difficult to explore in depth here, is the future of U.S. bilateral military relationships and alliances in Asia. Of particular concern are the U.S.-Korean relationship in the event of a democratic reunified peninsula and the still close, yet confusing, U.S. relationship with Taiwan.

The prevailing U.S. mind-set that worries about checking other potential great powers such as China might be expected to prefer that the United States remain allied with Korea after a possible reunification. China would probably object to such a move, seeing it as proof of a U.S. hegemonic outlook that preferred to maintain a global military presence and capability even when clear rationales for that capability were not persuasively articulated. Without a North Korean threat, the U.S. presence would be difficult to justify, particularly in light of the presumed availability of Japanese bases to provide the United States with naval and air access to most of Asia for peace operations or crisis response.

Of course, Japan might not be as good a base as Korea for any crisis-response activities involving China or Russia. Therein lies the problem, from the perspective of Beijing. As with NATO expansion against a remote and hypothetical Russian threat to central Europe, a U.S. decision to keep a strong bilateral military alliance with Korea—particularly one involving a U.S. military presence—could be interpreted as a confrontational pose. China also could be expected to view it as an affront to its legitimate interests in its immediate neighborhood; the United States clearly would not and has not tolerated such a move from some other power near its own borders. Acting in such a manner might be acceptable for a world in which the United States could sustain both overwhelming global military dominance and the will to exercise that dominance. But it may not meet either of those conditions indefinitely into the twenty-first century (if indeed it even does today), particularly near Chinese borders.

Turning to Taiwan, that country is at much greater near-term risk from Chinese attack than any reunified Korea would be. In addition, the United States has made security pledges to Taiwan, though the depth of its commitment is unclear and for that reason potentially dangerous.[23] How should the United States handle its ongoing relationship with Taiwan in a post–cold war era?

The United States would be well served to continue supporting a resolution of the Taiwan-China standoff that is mutually acceptable to both sides, implying opposition to a mainland Chinese invasion on the one hand and a unilateral declaration of Taiwanese independence on the other.[24] Such a policy is likely to allow the United States to navigate a difficult path whose opposing edges—reneging on a commitment to Taiwan or fighting China over Taiwan—are both highly undesirable. But it is worth emphasizing that the latter possibility is far more dangerous. It would entail challenging the world's chief rising power over a matter entailing asymmetrical sets of interests on the part of China and the United States, in a situation where two of the three countries involved possess nuclear weapons. China cannot expect the world to view its relationship with Taiwan as a purely internal matter. But neither should the world view it as a fair barometer of the future course of Chinese attitudes toward its neighbors in general, or view any Chinese conflict with Taiwan as one that necessarily requires full Western armed opposition.

The appropriate U.S. tools for addressing any blatant Chinese aggression against Taiwan include instituting a wide range of international economic sanctions and keeping bans on trade and financial flows in place for a significant number of years. They may also extend to the lesser military step of helping Taiwan break a blockade imposed by China. The latter recourse may not be sustainable into the heart of the twenty-first century, when China may be sufficiently technologically advanced to take full advantage of its geographic proximity and challenge the U.S. Navy in Taiwanese waters. But the problem seems likely to be solved by then, particularly as the partisans of the Chinese civil war on both sides die and are replaced by a new generation of leaders and voters.   •

Arms Export Policies

If the defense budget debate is rather remarkable for its narrow zone of differences, the thinking on arms sales is even more so. Certain advocacy groups oppose most sales on principle, but most security analysts seem to favor them generally and to be uninterested in considering specific policies for restraint.[25] After nearly two years of policy review, the Clinton administration has now produced a plan for selling arms overseas that is meeting little resistance. Preserving most of the basic thrust of Bush administration and early Clinton administration policy, the plan puts an additional emphasis on the commercial advantages of such sales and in particular on their benefits for maintaining the U.S. defense industrial base.[26]

The degree to which such a doctrine is being condoned and supported by the security community is remarkable in light of the fact that the recent U.S. sale of 150 F-16 fighters to Taiwan, while in part a response to Chinese acquisition of a much smaller number of Su-27 fighters from Russia, flew directly in the face of a standing U.S. commitment to Beijing. Similarly, the sale of 72 F-15 fighters to Saudi Arabia—together with sales of ground equipment, Patriot missiles, and additional assets to that country and other Persian Gulf states—contradicted a considerable amount of high-level U.S. rhetoric after the Gulf War about the need to introduce restraint into the Mideast arms market. Those sales may also be weakening the U.S. effort to limit other countries' sales to Iran and keep sanctions on Iraq.[27] Yet serious efforts to control the size of regional threats could have significant benefits for the U.S. defense budget and perhaps also the likelihood and scope of any future regional conflict.[28]

U.S. Arms Makers' Advantages

Commercial and domestic political factors in U.S. arms sales, witnessed in the announcement of the F-15 and F-16 sales during a presidential campaign, hardly need more encouragement or help.[29] The United States has already been able to capture more than half of the world arms market in recent years and is likely to retain such a share in the future.[30]

Although it is not unreasonable for U.S. weapons manufacturers to aspire to even higher levels of sales, their current market share is already quite high. The United States made 70 percent of the new arms export sales to developing countries in 1993 and is likely to retain a 55 to 60 percent market share in the future, far above its share of roughly one-quarter in the 1980s.[31] Despite precipitous drops in the overall levels of global military production and associated arms transactions, the United States is managing to maintain its arms sales near its past average of some $15 billion a year.[32]

U.S. arms manufacturers have several natural advantages over their competitors and should not protest too much about the few restrictions they face. The quality of their equipment benefits from a U.S. research and development budget several times that of Europe's aggregate level, and they are assured nearly $3 billion a year in arms sales to Egypt and Israel that are financed by the U.S. taxpayer through foreign aid programs. Furthermore, they are linked politically to the sole global superpower and only guarantor of regional stability in several parts of the world. Potential buyers have a strong incentive to curry favor with the U.S. government by buying American arms and can thereby also enhance the prospects for interoperability with any outside force that might someday come to their defense.

But these built-in advantages should not be expected to yield U.S. firms anything close to 100 percent of the global market, even in places outside of Europe, Iran, Iraq, North Korea, and Libya. The same type of political and security logic that tends to give U.S. firms something of an advantage also means that many buyers, such as Saudi Arabia and Kuwait, will prefer to diversify their supplier bases to a certain degree. By doing so, they improve their prospects for garnering broad international support among members of the UN Security Council and other important countries should crises develop that require multilateral attention.[33]

Arms Sales and U.S-China Relations

By selling 150 F-16s to Taiwan, particularly given the timing of the decision (and its endorsement by candidate Clinton) during a presidential race in which electoral votes from states that produce F-16s were of critical importance, the United States displayed the same type of economic nationalism that it often accuses China itself of pursuing. It thereby provided Beijing with a tailor-made excuse for continuing arms export policies with which the United States does not concur and handicapped the prospects for U.S. efforts to get China to provide more information on its military forces, plans, and budgets. If China is convinced that the United States is interested first and foremost in promoting its own interests and damaging China's, it will naturally see efforts at openness, such as those of Secretary Perry in October 1994, to be unfriendly prying into its own affairs.[34] China's cooperation as a producer of arms and nuclear and missile technologies is too important to jeopardize over a few hundred million dollars in U.S. profits. Its military restraint in dealings with Taiwan is also too important to risk jeopardizing by a giant arms sale at odds with a decade-old U.S. policy.

Arms Sales and Mideast Security

The Bush administration initiated discussions among the five permanent members of the UN Security Council to restrain sales to the Middle

East after the Persian Gulf war.[35] Countries there have as much inherent right to self-defense capabilities as any other. But some of those countries have temporarily forfeited that right by recent aggressive behavior. Other countries—notably, U.S. friends on the Arabian peninsula—are unlikely ever to develop defenses capable of doing more than slowing an initial encroachment of enemy forces, as acknowledged by former Defense Secretary Dick Cheney.[36] They will continue to depend on the United States for the lion's share of any effort to stanch a major threat to their security.

What of Russian arms sales to Iran, currently the main arms sales problem on U.S. minds? Iran is at present considerably weaker than Iraq, at least as measured in major weapons holdings, and far weaker than was pre-war Iraq; it is also substantially weaker than the more distant powers of Israel, Egypt, and Syria.[37] Its present pace of arms acquisitions, on the order of $1.5 billion a year and holding steady or declining, will hardly suffice to change that situation in a region where arms acquisitions by the major powers have often occurred at twice that rate.[38] Given that arms sales play a greater macroeconomic role in Russia than in this country, it is probably infeasible to expect to stop each and every Russian arms sale to Iran.[39]

Iranian state-sponsored terrorism and pursuit of weapons of mass destruction constitute serious dangers to the West and have no justifiable purpose as instruments of national self-defense, but those same conclusions do not apply to Iran's acquisition of basic conventional self-defense capabilities. To take a specific example, Iranian acquisition of submarines may be undesirable from a Western perspective and of concern given Iran's past willingness to harass Gulf commercial traffic. It would therefore be welcome if transfers of submarines to Iran could be stopped. But there is no strong stigma against the transfer of submarines in the world today, and for good reason: weapons of mass destruction represent a much more profound security threat than attack submarines. It would thus seem inappropriate and counterproductive for the United States to harp too strongly or publicly on this issue—particularly in light of the fact that other countries have qualms about Washington's focus on Iran and are unlikely to support the United States on all matters concerning Teheran.[40]

Focusing nonproliferation policy exclusively on the countries on the U.S. terrorist list—particularly Iran, Iraq, and Libya—is a bit artificial in that some of the Gulf Cooperation Council regimes are arguably little better from a broad democracy and human rights perspective. They probably are less militarily threatening to their neighbors than Iran, Iraq, and Libya, and less guilty (though not innocent) of support for extremist and terrorist groups. And Iran and Iraq can paint fairly plausible cases that they face serious threats (each other and, to a degree, Syria) that justify their rearmament programs.

A sensible remedy to the Mideast arms transfer problem would be to cast a more skeptical eye on arms sales to nondemocratic regimes, in keeping with guidelines suggested in 1993 and again in 1995 by Representative Cynthia McKinney and Senator Mark Hatfield. In applying that approach to the Persian Gulf region, the world's major arms exporters should agree not to sell arms when doing so would make any country's inventory of a major weapons system exceed the current holdings of Iraq, still the best-armed of the Persian Gulf states.[41] They should also generally avoid arming countries at rates higher than would be consistent with maintaining an arsenal the size of Iraq's over the typical lifetime of major combat equipment—roughly twenty-five to thirty years. Although such a framework would admittedly be somewhat arbitrary, it would have a basic economic logic in that curtailing arsenals to that size or less would probably reduce regional spending on defense by half, to about 5 percent of GDP. This would be roughly consistent with the suggestions of recent World Bank Presidents Robert McNamara and Barber Conable.[42] Thus, in order to keep the tank holdings of individual national armies under 2,000, for example, annual deliveries could not exceed 70 or so. In order to avoid a qualitative arms race that might naturally result from such quantitative limits, supplier countries could also respect a rough limit of $1 billion a year on their combined deliveries to any given country in the region.[43]

Such a policy would avoid fissures with Russia over its relatively modest sales of arms to Iran, establish a framework for dealing with Iraq in any postsanctions era, and allow Pentagon planners—as well as Congress and the U.S. taxpayer—to worry less about the possibility of another Desert Storm–like war in the Middle East. Under such an approach, a future regional adversary might have only one-third the equipment inventories and one-half the overall strength of prewar Iraq.

Participation by the permanent members of the UN Security Council and all other members of NATO would provide a very strong basis for such a supplier arrangement. Despite the warnings of some that the proliferation of conventional arms production capability is accelerating, industrialized countries continue to export more than 90 percent of the world's arms as measured by value, a level unchanged from a decade earlier.[44] (By contrast, the major powers may not be able to prevent the spread of small arms and lower-quality mortars and the like).[45]

Conclusion

The policies I suggest in this book would produce a U.S. military that stayed capable against near-term plausible threats to key U.S. interests and engaged in multilateral security activities more generally, but that otherwise relinquished a certain amount of its overwhelming advantage. Capabilities for regional military conflicts would be changed to ensure the defense of Korea and Southwest Asia at lower cost and higher probability of deterring conflict or containing it quickly. Substantial U.S. militarily involvement elsewhere would not be precluded. But becoming involved in two conflicts at once in other regions would be judged highly unlikely and probably ill advised, as would taking on China or Russia militarily over most types of territorial and border disputes in those states' neighborhoods. The global presence doctrine that had a certain logic when Moscow was the target audience would be replaced by greater flexibility and fewer routine patrols, particularly when the U.S. military was actively involved in multilateral security activities. Nuclear weapons would be increasingly recognized as an international security scourge and downgraded in U.S. military posture. Efforts would be made to cooperate with close allies in force planning for the most likely regional contingencies, to improve military-to-military ties with Russia and China (ultimately including activities such as joint naval patrols), and to help other countries improve their capabilities to assist in UN peace operations.

Would the sum total of these policy changes make a fundamental difference in how U.S. security policy was perceived overseas? Would it improve the likelihood that Russia, China, and other countries would decide to pursue cooperation rather than conflict with the West in general and the United States in particular? It is difficult to know. But ensuring that the short-term imperatives of security are met while endeavoring to shape a viable global security architecture for the next century must be preferable to perpetuating many cold war patterns of behavior by default. Combining strength and resolve with vision and inclusion would also be a much more fitting way to honor the legacy of twentieth-century U.S.

security policymakers, who combined altruism, enlightened self-interest, and multilateral military preparedness to shape the most successful security institutions in world history. Rather than a preoccupation with power, a similar blend of principles adapted to a new world is called for now.

Notes

1. On the changing nature of the international economic order, see Robert Gilpin, *The Political Economy of International Relations* (Princeton University Press, 1987); and Paul Kennedy, *The Rise and Fall of the Great Powers* (Random House, 1987). For a useful discussion of trends in Asia, see Aaron L. Friedberg, "Ripe for Rivalry: Prospects for Peace in a Multipolar Asia," *International Security*, vol. 18 (Winter 1993–1994), pp. 5–33.

2. As Richard Betts dispassionately writes, "So should we want China to get rich or not? For liberals, the answer is yes, since a quarter of the world's people would be relieved from poverty and because economic growth should make democratization more likely, which in turn should prevent war between Beijing and other democracies. For realists, the answer should be no, since a rich China would overturn any balance of power. But what can we do about it anyway? American leverage on Beijing after the cold war is not overwhelming. . . . As with all too many of the problems of security in East Asia, we may begin with a realist diagnosis but be forced into banking on liberal solutions, simply because the costs of controlling the balance of power may be too high." See Richard K. Betts, "Wealth, Power, and Instability: East Asia and the United States after the Cold War," *International Security*, vol. 18 (Winter 1993–1994), p. 55. See also John Lewis Gaddis, "International Relations Theory and the End of the Cold War," *International Security*, vol. 17 (Winter 1992–1993), pp. 5–58.

3. McGeorge Bundy, *Danger and Survival* (Vintage Books, 1988); Kennedy, *Rise and Fall of the Great Powers*; Richard H. Ullman, *Securing Europe* (Princeton University Press, 1991); John Mueller, "The Essential Irrelevance of Nuclear Weapons: Stability in the Postwar World," *International Security*, vol. 13 (Fall 1988), pp. 55–68; Michael W. Doyle, "Liberalism and World Politics," *American Political Science Review*, vol. 80 (December 1986), pp. 1151–69; and Stephen Van Evera, "Primed for Peace: Europe after the Cold War," *International Security*, vol. 15 (Winter 1990–1991), pp. 7–57.

4. See, for example, Kenneth N. Waltz, *Theory of International Politics* (Random House, 1979).

5. For a similar view, see Michael E. Brown, "NATO Expansion: Wait and See," *Washington Post*, December 26, 1994, p. A29.

6. See Richard K. Betts, "Systems for Peace or Causes of War? Collective Security, Arms Control, and the New Europe," *International Security*, vol. 17 (Summer 1992), p. 36.

7. An example of the type of scholarship that demands Russia not act with any signs of great-power interest comes from Henry Kissinger: "Of course, Russia must be given every opportunity for a truly cooperative relationship. But not at the cost of tempting Russian expansionism by removing the obstacles to it. Even the presumably reformist Yeltsin government has insisted on an assertive superpower role by throwing

its weight around." See "Expand NATO Now," *Washington Post*, December 19, 1994, p. A27.

8. R. James Woolsey, director of Central Intelligence, statement for the record to the Senate Select Committee on Intelligence, January 10, 1995, pp. 26–27.

9. See Steven Erlanger, "Dire Warnings for Parliament on State of Russian Army," *New York Times*, November 19, 1994; John D. Steinbruner, "Reluctant Strategic Realignment: The Need for a New View of National Security," *Brookings Review*, vol. 13 (Winter 1995), pp. 4–9; Woolsey, statement for the record, January 10, 1995, p. 24; and John Pomfret, "Russia Accused of Impeding Uranium-Smuggling Probe," *Washington Post*, February 12, 1995, p. A39.

10. Jeff Gerth, "In a Furtive, Frantic Market, America Buys Russian Arms," *New York Times*, December 24, 1994, p. A1; and statement of Louis J. Freeh, director of the Federal Bureau of Investigation, before the Subcommittee on Investigations, Senate Committee on Governmental Affairs, May 25, 1994, pp. 1–4.

11. See R. Jeffrey Smith, "Danger Is Seen in Rapid NATO Expansion," *Washington Post*, November 23, 1994, p. A16.

12. See Steven Greenhouse, "Ukraine Votes to Become a Nuclear-Free Country," *New York Times*, November 17, 1994, p. A10.

13. For a good description of the Soviet mind-set during that era, see Raymond L. Garthoff, *Detente and Confrontation*, rev. ed. (Brookings, 1994), pp. 1152–74.

14. See Charles J. Dick, "The Military Doctrine of the Russian Federation," *Journal of Slavic Military Studies*, vol. 7 (September 1994), pp. 497–99; and Alexei Arbatov and analysts from the Russian Air Force, "Russian Air Strategy and Combat Aircraft Production: A Russian Air Force View," in Randall Forsberg, ed., *The Arms Production Dilemma: Contraction and Restraint in the World Combat Aircraft Industry* (MIT Press, 1994), pp. 17–60.

15. See Steinbruner, "Reluctant Strategic Realignment."

16. Elaine Sciolino, "Yeltsin Says NATO Is Trying to Split Continent Again," *New York Times*, December 6, 1994, p. A1.

17. Fred C. Iklé, "How to Ruin NATO," *New York Times*, January 11, 1995, p. A21.

18. See Zbigniew Brzezinski, "NATO—Expand or Die?" *New York Times*, December 28, 1994, p. A15.

19. See R. Jeffrey Smith and Daniel Williams, "Russia Intends to Pursue Guarantees from NATO," *Washington Post*, March 11, 1995, p. A21; and Julia Preston, "Russia Shows Testy New Assertiveness at UN," *Washington Post*, December 29, 1994, p. 20.

20. See for example, Willy Claes, secretary-general of NATO, "Security Still Rests in NATO," *Defense News*, November 21–27, 1994, p. 19.

21. Attitudes in Germany have changed substantially of late, but until an actual war occurs it will be difficult to know how deeply the changes have penetrated society. German contributions to a multilateral warfighting force could be substantial; as one German general writes, "It will therefore suffice to maintain a contingent with the size of a present-day Army division, plus the relevant Air Force and Navy elements. We aim at getting such a contingent ready for deployment to any place at a 15 to 30 days notice by the year 2000." See General Klaus Naumann, chief of staff of German Federal Armed Forces, "German Security Policy and Future Tasks of the *Bundeswehr*," *RUSI Journal*, vol. 139 (December 1994), pp. 8–13.

22. See Bob Furlong, "Eurocorps Counts Down to 1995 Launch," *International Defense Review*, vol. 27 (November 1994), pp. 30–38.

23. See Betts, "Wealth, Power, and Instability," p. 67.

24. Harry Harding, *A Fragile Relationship* (Brookings, 1992), pp. 345–50.

25. For two exceptions to this trend, see Congressional Budget Office, *Limiting Conventional Arms Exports to the Middle East* (September 1992); and Forsberg, ed., *Arms Production Dilemma*.

26. Ralph Vartabedian and John M. Broder, "U.S. Weighs New Arms Sales Policy," *Los Angeles Times*, November 15, 1994, p. 1.

27. Harding, *Fragile Relationship*, p. 384; and CBO, *Limiting Conventional Arms Exports to the Middle East*, pp. 3–24.

28. CBO, *Limiting Conventional Arms Exports to the Middle East*, p. 72.

29. For another view that such a commercial, defense-industrial base rationale has already become commonplace, see Office of Technology Assessment, *Global Arms Trade: Commerce in Advanced Military Technology and Weapons* (June 1991), p. 13.

30. Office of the Secretary of Defense, "World-Wide Conventional Arms Trade (1994–2000): A Forecast and Analysis," December 1994, p. v.

31. CBO, *Limiting Conventional Arms Exports to the Middle East*, pp. 11–12; Arms Control and Disarmament Agency, *World Military Expenditures and Arms Transfers, 1991–1992* (Government Printing Office, 1994), p. 14; and Department of Defense, *World-Wide Conventional Arms Trade (1994–2000)* (December 1994).

32. "U.S. Arms Policy in Firing Line," *London Financial Times*, November 17, 1994, p. 5; Richard F. Grimmett, "Conventional Arms Transfers to the Third World, 1986–1993," Congressional Research Service, July 29, 1994, pp. 55–56; and Department of Defense news briefing by Kenneth H. Bacon, assistant to the secretary of defense for public affairs, November 15, 1994.

33. See Philip Finnegan, "Kuwait to Continue Diversification in Arms Buys," *Defense News*, November 28–December 4, 1994, p. 3; and Peter Sincock, "Moving Along, But Not Yet in Step," *International Defense Review*, vol. 27 (December 1994), p. 36.

34. Michael R. Gordon, "U.S. to China: Be More Open on Arms Plan," *New York Times*, October 19, 1994, p. 14.

35. See Alan Platt, ed., "Report of the Study Group on Multilateral Arms Transfer Guidelines for the Middle East" (Washington: Henry L. Stimson Center, 1992), p. 4.

36. David B. Ottaway, "U.S., Saudis to Study Long-Term Defense Needs of Gulf Region," *Washington Post*, April 21, 1991, p. A26.

37. CBO, *Limiting Conventional Arms Exports to the Middle East*, pp. 82–84.

38. Grimmett, "Conventional Arms Transfers to the Third World, 1986–1993," pp. 58–59, 69–70; and CBO, *Limiting Conventional Arms Exports to the Middle East*, p. 9.

39. Randall Forsberg and Jonathan Cohen, "Issues and Choices in Arms Production and Trade," in Forsberg, ed., *Arms Production Dilemma*, p. 280; and Barbara Opall, "Russian-Iran Sales Hinder 23-Nation Export Guideline," *Defense News*, February 20–26, 1995, p. 1.

40. See "Post-Cocom Meeting Fruitless as Russian Sales to Iran Dominate Debate," *Inside the Pentagon*, December 22, 1994, p. 5; and "Meeting Stirs Little Hope for Completion of Post-Cocom Agreement," *Inside the Pentagon*, December 8, 1994, p. 5.

41. See Michael O'Hanlon, "Limiting Conventional Arms Sales to the Persian Gulf," in James Brown, ed., *New Horizons and Challenges in Arms Control and*

Verification (Amsterdam: VU University Press, 1994), pp. 104–05; and Platt, ed., "Report of the Study Group on Multilateral Arms Transfer Guidelines," p. 43.

42. See CBO, *Limiting Conventional Arms Exports to the Middle East*, p. 39.

43. Ibid., pp. 31–45.

44. See OTA, *Global Arms Trade*, pp. 3–16; Richard A. Bitzinger, "The Globalization of the Arms Industry: The Next Proliferation Challenge," International Security, vol. 19 (Fall 1994), pp. 170–98; and ACDA, *World Military Expenditures and Arms Transfers*, p. 14.

45. See, for example, W. Seth Carus, *Cruise Missile Proliferation in the 1990s* (Westport, Conn.: Praeger, 1992), pp. xv–xvi.

LANCHESTER AND DUPUY EQUATIONS

ALTHOUGH THE BASIC IDEAS that undergird the well-known Lanchester and Dupuy equations are straightforward and not dissimilar from the techniques used in chapter 3, it may be useful to summarize the mathematics of those well-known approaches here as well.

Lanchester Equations

Lanchester equations link casualty and attrition rates to target acquisition, fire rates, and weapons effectiveness on two sides of a battle. They do not generally account for different types of weapons; nor do they provide any insight into the interactions between airpower and ground combat or the effects of movement, distance, weather, countermeasures, tactics, or other basic physical characteristics of an actual battle.[1]

However, Lanchester equations can still prove useful if relevant data from past wars are available with which to "normalize" or standardize the equations. Assuming similar weapons characteristics and similar dynamics of engagement in a future war, the equations can provide useful insight.[2] The so-called square law form, corresponding to situations where most equipment and personnel are lost as a result of direct fire at specific enemy targets (rather than simple barrage, use of minefields, or other weapons and tactics where the concentration of an army's force affects its own casualty rates) is the most applicable form for most types of combat involving precision-delivery munitions.[3] Its basic form is as follows:

$$b[B(0)^2 - B(t)^2] = r[R(0)^2 - R(t)^2].$$

In that equation, B and R are the force levels at time 0 and t (that is, initial force levels and levels at some later time), respectively. The symbols *b* and *r* are measures of destructiveness per unit time for those same forces; that is, *b* indicates the effectiveness of *B* in destroying *R*. The basic differential equations from which the above equation is derived are:

$$dR(t)/dt = -bB(t)$$
$$dB(t)/dt = -rR(t).$$

Lanchester equations are a commonsensical representation of the basic fact that more gunners shooting better weapons will produce more casualties, or to be precise, more attrition to fighting capability, whatever it may be composed of. The hard work is clearly in estimating the coefficients *b* and *r* and finding appropriate units with which to represent *B* and *R*, however.

Actually, these equations should be matrix equations for modern militaries, composed as they are of a wide variety of weapons platforms with various armaments. Such a complete representation would still beg the question of estimating coefficients, of which there would be many more. It would also not allow for the fact that different weapons of the same type would be firing from different distances with different effectiveness. To broach such complexity in a mathematically rigorous way, a major computer model and reliable databases on the battlefield performance of all relevant weapons systems would be needed. But the simple form of Lanchester equations can provide an order-of-magnitude estimate useful for some purposes.

This approach was recently employed by William Kaufmann of Brookings to assess the likely outcome of a future war similar to Desert Storm but at different force levels.[4] Using a somewhat different representation of the Lanchester equations, he assigned a factor-of-3 firepower advantage to allied forces, meaning that at the outbreak of the 1991 ground war their 12 divisions had a score of 36 to Iraq's 21 (the actual number of divisions that Iraq had remaining at that time). Kaufmann then calculated that the results of that war were consistent with a factor-of-12 allied advantage in overall military effectiveness; that is, the parameter tied to the lower-case coefficients in the Lanchester laws. Such a factor is not surprising in light of specific data available from the war, such as exchange ratios on the order of 100:1 for tank-to-tank warfare.

Showing such a calculation in terms of Lanchester's law, and assuming that the war continues until only 3 Iraqi divisions are left, as Kaufmann does, one gets:

$$B(t) = \{[r/b][R(t)^2 - R(0)^2] + B(0)\}^{1/2}$$
$$= \{[1/12] [9 - 441] + 1,296\}^{1/2}$$
$$= 35.5 \text{ divisions.}$$

Allocating losses proportionately to U.S. and allied forces based on the sizes of their relative contributions implies that about 0.35 U.S. division-equivalents, or 0.12 actual divisions, are lost. Taking Kaufmann's estimate that equipment is lost four times as fast as people (relative to their initial levels), that one-fourth of all casualties are deaths, and that 17,000 individuals comprise a U.S. heavy division, one obtains 120 U.S. deaths in the ground battle—close to the actual number.

But in fact Iraq did not lose such a high percentage of its forces in the Gulf War. By an alternative calculation that assumes ground combat to be responsible for the destruction of only 10 Iraqi divisions in ground combat, 35.6 allied division equivalents would remain once combat ceased, corresponding to a loss of roughly 0.09 U.S. divisions, or 90 U.S. deaths. Thus, even after adjusting for a more modest allied ground war victory, as now seems to have been the case given the decision not to destroy much of the Republican Guard, the effectiveness parameter of about 12 used by Kaufmann appears a reasonable approximation.

Dupuy Method

After retiring from the Army, Colonel Trevor Dupuy assembled a great body of data on warfare from which he devised some simple rules of thumb. Although he is less famous than Lanchester, his mathematics are little different, and the database on which he draws is far more modern than that of the British engineer. Moreover, the data allow for estimates not only of relative casualty rates but also of the losses of tanks, artillery, and other equipment. The predictive ability of his or any other model based on historical data should always be questioned, but the reasonable success of his approach in predicting an overwhelming and low-casualty coalition victory in the Gulf—based as it was on extrapolation from data from Arab-Israeli wars and other relevant experience—shows the value of using historically tested simple equations to get a feeling for future conflicts.[5]

Dupuy provides, among other things, data that can help one estimate the advantages of fighting on the tactical defensive with the aid of militarily desirable terrain. To some degree, the traditional preference for fighting from prepared positions is to gain the advantage of first shot and defensive shielding that U.S. forces today typically enjoy anyway by virtue of their vastly superior links to overhead reconnaissance systems, the sensors on individual combat platforms, and the proficiency of troops. But added advantages can be gained by forcing an adversary to traverse difficult terrain, particularly if mines and obstacles are employed. This type of approach is of most relevance to the Korean theater.

Dupuy's formula for a military's daily personnel casualty rates is a linear expression that multiplies the military's personnel strength by its relative combat capability—typically, firepower per person times the effectiveness of that firepower per person. It also factors in weather, terrain, defensive preparation, and surprise by coefficients that typically range between 0.5 and 1.5. Dupuy's data allow him to estimate the latter parameters from historical experience, but he must rely on the overall outcomes of previous wars to make estimates for relative combat capability.[6]

For the Gulf War, Dupuy estimated that U.S. forces contained 3 times as much raw capability as did Iraqi forces, on a divisional basis, and that the product of their mobility with their other capabilities would produce another factor-of-3 advantage. Arab forces were assumed to represent a force that effectively would augment the size of the U.S. force by about another 15 percent. Mitigating these advantages, whose combined effect was a factor-of-10 superiority for the coalition, was the superior number of Iraqi divisions—25 versus the U.S. total of 10, as well as the Iraqi advantage in fighting on the defensive from prepared positions, which was assumed to provide a doubling of Iraqi capability. Thus, the net coalition advantage was about a factor of 2. Since casualty rates are proportional both to disparities in overall force effectiveness as well as one's own personnel levels on the battlefield, the casualty ratio in the U.S. favor was calculated to be a factor of about 6.[7]

Actual casualty ratios were probably more on the order of 100:1. Thus it seems that Dupuy's formulation either did not give proper due to U.S. technological and training advantages that exceeded even what the Israelis possessed in earlier Mideast wars, or that his approach does not allow for the type of catastrophic breakdown in one side's force that can be produced by a major tactical success by the other side.

Notes

1. Joshua M. Epstein, *Strategy and Force Planning: The Case of the Persian Gulf* (Brookings, 1987), pp. 146–55.

2. See William W. Kaufmann, *Assessing the Base Force: How Much Is Too Much?* (Brookings, 1992), pp. 94–97.

3. Epstein, *Strategy and Force Planning*, p. 146.

4. Kaufmann, *Assessing the Base Force*, pp. 53–57, 94–97.

5. See Trevor N. Dupuy, *If War Comes . . . How To Defeat Saddam Hussein* (McLean, Va.: HERO Books, 1991), p. 104.

6. Trevor N. Dupuy, *Attrition: Forecasting Battle Casualties and Equipment Losses in Modern War* (McLean, Va.: HERO Books, 1990), pp. 104–152.

7. Dupuy, *Attrition*, pp. 128–31.

CONVENTIONAL BOMBERS IN REGIONAL WARFARE

SECURITY POLICYMAKERS have become intrigued with the notion of responding to a sudden outbreak of regional warfare by making greater use of heavy bombers—the B-1, B-2, and B-52 fleets—flying out of U.S. bases or other locations not immediately contiguous to the zone of conflict. Doing so has been made possible by the stealthier capabilities of the B-1 and particularly the B-2, which may permit lower-altitude unescorted flight; by the anticipated development of new, advanced munitions with either inertial guidance or homing capabilities, permitting accurate bombing from higher altitude than is now the case; and by planned electronic and sensor upgrades to the B-1 and B-52 aircraft to permit them to deliver such munitions after locating appropriate targets.[1]

The BUR document, upon its publication in October 1993, viewed a 100-bomber fleet as a basic building block for fighting a single major regional contingency. The two-war strategy of the BUR would thus have seemed to require some 200 bombers, broadly consistent with the force structure proposal made in that document for "up to 184" heavy bombers. A final decision was made contingent on the then ongoing nuclear posture review. However, fiscal realities interceded, and the administration's plan now envisions a force in the neighborhood of 150 planes once all 20 B-2s are completed and deployed. This decision implies that bombers, especially important early in a conflict, could be "swung" from one theater to another and thereby provide 100 bombers to both warfighting commanders—provided, of course, that the wars were only "nearly simultaneous."[2] (In Desert Storm, about 70 B-52 aircraft simply delivered unguided bombs from high altitudes in imprecise carpet-bombing operations, and some thirty-five cruise missiles were also delivered by bomber aircraft during that war.)[3]

In considering the potential role of bombers in future U.S. combat operations, three central and conflicting points need to be made right away. First, the theoretical potential of bombers equipped with next-generation precision-guided munitions is indeed great and does not depend on the availability of local airfields. But second, the practical challenges to realizing that potential are enormous: developing reliable and effective munitions that are difficult for an enemy to counter; safely finding, identifying, and tracking targets in a tactical setting without escort by fighter or command-and-control aircraft; and making sufficiently rapid political decisions to undertake major combat operations against an aggressor in the immediate aftermath of its decision to attack. Third and most important, Secretary Perry's resistance to reopening the issue of B-2 production seems well founded, given the proven ability of tactical combat aircraft to carry out precision-strike missions effectively and likely availability of regional airfields for the potential conflicts of greatest concern to the United States.[4] The United States would probably be better served to improve, principally through pre-positioning, airlift, and tanker aircraft, its abilities to deploy and then employ tactical air superiority and attack aircraft quickly. They are proven in such missions; by contrast, bombers are not.

Under the Air Force's 1992 bomber roadmap approach, bombers would first acquire more precise and lethal capabilities for attacks against fixed, strategic targets. The first round of improved munitions would feature the joint-direct attack munition (JDAM), the early version of which would have inertial guidance updated by global positioning system receivers. Lacking homing devices, they would be used primarily against fixed targets. Those might include fixed surface-to-air missile sites, bridges, key factories, airfields, depots, communications centers, railroad switching stations, and military staging areas. According to the Air Force, and consistent with General Charles Horner's initial list of some 200 top-priority targets for the air war against Iraq, perhaps 1,250 aim-points would be attacked (several per target), with a goal of destroying the vast majority within five days.[5]

Consider the dynamics of a bomber war in which B-2 aircraft were reserved for antiarmor attacks. Over the five-day period, the average B-1 or B-52 aircraft might fly either one or two roundtrips against fixed targets, making for a total of, say, 200 sorties. Assuming that 16 munitions would be carried by each aircraft, those figures would imply an average of about 2.5 munitions per aimpoint. B-52s would conduct direct attack against less defended, low-threat targets and standoff attacks against medium-threat sites; B-1s would use standoff attacks against heavily defended high-threat sites and either standoff or direct attacks against other categories of enemy assets.[6] These types of bomber attacks may work, though it remains doubtful that a commander would authorize them without first establishing air superiority with tactical aircraft.

What of the antiarmor mission? Here, due to the need to overfly enemy forces in close proximity, the B-2 bomber is generally the platform of interest. The arithmetic presented by the RAND Corporation and other advocates of airpower is seducing. For example, a bomber could carry perhaps thirty-two joint standoff weapons, each of which might contain twenty to forty submunitions with infrared homing devices. This means that, even if it took five or more munitions to destroy a given vehicle, a three-bomber force could contain enough firepower in a single load to stop an entire armored division with more than 1,000 vehicles. In order to account for the possibility of the dispersal of a tank force, the uncertainty about when armored columns would be moved by an adversary, and the distances involved in bombing operations based out of the United States, RAND suggests that sixty bombers might be needed to stop a ten-division assault over a ten-day period.[7]

Do these calculations hold up? They may, but there are reasons to think that they are very optimistic and leave the burden of proof on those who would argue for more bombers. For example, to acquire targets, the B-2 presumably would need to use its radar—thereby potentially surrendering the very stealth that would allegedly make it possible to send billion-dollar airplanes unescorted into highly hostile airspace—or would need to hope for good weather in order to use optical or infrared sensors.[8] Simply getting within range to make a single release of munitions, which would have ranges of several tens of kilometers, would be hard enough. Doing so in several different places in order to attack dispersed columns would make survivability all the more difficult, especially since the aggressor could surge tactical aircraft and put air-defense radars on high alert during periods of any intense movement of its armored columns.[9]

The unlikelihood of finding targets and delivering ordnance without incurring substantial attrition to the bomber force is what led General John Chain, then commander of the Strategic Air Command, to argue in 1990 that "because of the value of the [B-2], I can't see putting very many at risk in a conventional conflict."[10] His opinion may have changed in light of today's much lower nuclear-related demands upon the B-2 force and the hope for more capable stand-off munitions, but it remains telling.

Finally, sensors would need to cope with any decoys, jammers, or other countermeasures that might be present. The uncertainties associated with bombers themselves would also have their counterparts in the munitions, guided by small, infrared homing devices that would need to acquire and then destroy targets that might themselves be able to deploy flares or other protection.

Perhaps even more strikingly, there is the matter of cost: procuring an additional twenty B-2 bombers and assorted spare parts and the like would probably cost $20 billion to $26 billion at this point, and procuring forty more might therefore cost roughly $35 billion to $50 billion.[11] In addition, operating and maintenance costs could well prove greater than expected, perhaps approaching a billion dollars a year for an additional forty planes.[12] That price tag for destroying ten divisions with B-2s is in stark economic contrast to the capability of existing tactical combat forces to execute the same mission much more cheaply. As discussed in chapter 3, doing so within ten days would require a one-time investment of $10 billion for sixty added KC-10 tankers or the equivalent capacity in a similar aircraft. (There would be additional costs for pre-positioned munitions, equipment, and fuel, but the B-2 fleet would also require such additional expenses.) The added tankers would have additional military benefits above and beyond their role in deploying tactical combat aircraft, moreover, because they are also able to speed the deployment of other forces and supplies. Those tankers would cost only about $300 million dollars a year to operate. As argued in the text, they could ferry an eight- to ten-wing combat force to the theater of hostilities in one sortie, just as quickly as bombers could arrive.[13]

By relying on tactical combat aircraft, moreover, the United States would be establishing reliable air superiority as it engaged in sustained air-to-ground strikes. Whatever the allure of stealth and its theoretical capabilities to operate without electronic support or fighter escort, pilots flying into air defenses tend to like additional help—if the experience of the Gulf War, in which F-117 pilots requested and received jamming help from EF-111s, is any indication.[14]

On balance, the idea of using a B-2–led bomber force to provide very rapid responsiveness against major regional aggression seems to encounter too many uncertainties to merit large additional resources. But the idea of using today's bombers and cruise missiles to deliver precision-guided munitions from a distance should be considered. It would not put pilots or expensive aircraft at risk. At the cost of $2 million or so a cruise missile, and a loading of roughly sixteen sensor-fused weapons per cruise missile, this approach might allow a sizable fraction of a regional adversary's force to be destroyed for the cost of only $1 billion to $3 billion in cruise missiles.[15] It would require that some other platforms, perhaps unmanned aerial vehicles in tandem with high-altitude aircraft and satellites, provide targeting data. Such platforms are increasingly available. Still, when all is said and done, the U.S. tactical aircraft fleet has proven capability, is capable of self-protection, and can be made even more effective with selective and only moderately costly improvements in U.S. logistics and pre-positioning capabilities.

Notes

1. For useful descriptions of these basic Pentagon plans, see for example, Department of the Air Force, "The Bomber Roadmap: Enhancing the Nation's Conventional Bomber Force," (June 1992); Christopher Bowie and others, *The New Calculus: Analyzing Airpower's Changing Role in Joint Theater Campaigns* (Santa Monica, Calif.: RAND Corporation, 1993). The B-1 aircraft is also showing signs of getting beyond growing pains; see "B-1 Completes Six-Month Test with 84.3 Percent Readiness Rate," *Inside the Pentagon*, December 8, 1994, p. 4.

2. See General Jasper Welch, "Analysis of U.S. Requirements for Conventionally Armed Bombers," Northrop-Grumman Corporation, July 1994, p. 6. See also *Budget of the United States Government, Fiscal Year 1995*, p. 226; and Les Aspin, secretary of defense, *Annual Report to the President and the Congress* (January 1994), p. 187.

3. Department of Defense, *Conduct of the Persian Gulf War* (April 1992), pp. T-25–T-26.

4. Thomas E. Ricks and Jeff Cole, "Perry Opposes Renewing Work on Stealth Jet," *Wall Street Journal*, November 4, 1994, p. 1.

5. For an analysis along similar lines, see Joshua M. Epstein, "War with Iraq: What Price Victory?" Brookings Discussion Paper, January 10, 1991, p. 9. Ultimately, the United States attacked more than 700 strategic targets and some 3,000 aimpoints; see Bowie and others, *New Calculus*, p. 45.

6. Department of the Air Force, "Bomber Roadmap," pp. 3–7.

7. See, for example, Glenn C. Buchan, "The Use of Long-Range Bombers in a Changing World: A Classical Exercise in Systems Analysis," in Paul K. Davis, ed., *New Challenges for Defense Planning* (Santa Monica, Calif.: RAND Corporation, 1994), pp. 420–33.

8. David A. Perin, *A Comparison of Long-Range Bombers and Naval Forces* (Alexandria, Va.: Center for Naval Analyses, 1991), p. 31; Michael E. Brown, "The Case against the B–2," *International Security*, vol. 15 (Summer 1990), p. 133; and John Pike and David Bourns, *The Case against the Stealth Bomber* (Washington: Federation of American Scientists, 1988), p. 61.

9. See, for example, Michael Brower, *The B-2 Bomber: Impossible Cost, Dubious Mission* (Cambridge, Mass.: Union of Concerned Scientists, 1990), p. 12.

10. Ibid., p. 8.

11. Congressional Budget Office, "The Costs of the Administration's Plan for the Air Force through the Year 2010," CBO Memorandum, November 1994, p. 22; and John Boatman, "More B-2s not USAF Priority, says Gen. Loh," *Jane's Defence Weekly*, April 22, 1995, p. 14.

12. Brown, "The Case against the B-2," p. 147.

13. Sixty B-2s flying a round-trip mission would require most of today's KC-10 fleet: each bomber would require at least 2 KC-135A equivalents, or at least two-thirds of a KC-10 equivalent, so the entire mission would require at least 40 KC-10s out of the 60 in inventory. (During the era of high strategic nuclear alert, the U.S. bomber fleet of some 300 aircraft was supported by nearly 700 KC-135A equivalents, but on average the missions would probably have been somewhat more fuel-intensive than conventional bombing runs because of the need to fly at low altitudes over substantial amounts of Soviet territory. Thus the assumption of 2 KC-135A equivalents per bomber, for flights of comparable length, seems appropriate here.) See Congressional Budget Office, *Modernizing the Aerial Tanker Fleet: Prospects for Capacity, Timing, and Cost* (September 1985), pp. 4, 20.

14. Michael R. Gordon and Bernard E. Trainor, *The Generals' War: The Inside Story of the Conflict in the Gulf* (Little, Brown, 1995), pp. 118, 213.

15. See Robert Holzer, "New Munitions May Bolster Tomahawk," *Defense News*, October 17–23, 1994, p. 4; and Congressional Budget Office, *The START Treaty and Beyond* (October 1991), p. 139.